ISBN-13: 978-1495328794
ISBN-10: 1495328791

TABLE OF CONTENTS

INTRODUCTION

We live in the information age, which means that our problem is less one of obtaining information and more one of retaining and organizing all the quantities of information that we are required to ingest—both during our studies and afterwards. This we need to do to keep up with rapid changes in many fields and a continual influx of new information.

One of the recent techniques that have been devised to help us in this task is called Mind Mapping. A Mind Map is a diagram you create to organize your thoughts. In conventional note-taking, you write information down line by line or perhaps column by column. Mind Mapping differs from such note-taking in that you present the information more in the form of a diagram.

With the diagram, you start with a central key idea drawn in the center of the paper. Other thoughts related to the key idea are arranged radially around the center with lines branching out from the key idea to these subtopics to show that they are related to one another. Details related to each subtopic can be shown to be connected to it through more lines.

It looks something like this:

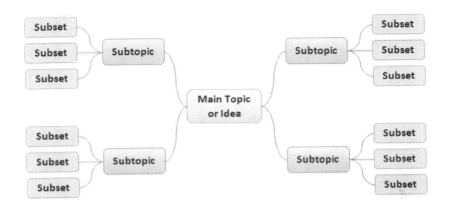

As you can see, you have the main topic in the middle, then the subtopics and their subsets branch out from that main idea.

Mind Maps function on the principle of *Radiant Thinking* (a term developed by Tony Buzan, an avid promoter of the technique). Radiant Thinking means our thoughts spread out indefinitely from a key central idea, as shown in the diagram above, which Buzan says is the natural and automatic way for humans to think.

Through Mind Mapping, we are able to capture on a flat surface the multidimensional reality of what it is we need to learn. In fact, different cortical skills come into play: line, form, color, visual rhythm, texture, dimension and particularly imagination. The graphic nature of this method produces more precise and powerful associations of ideas.

A Historical Overview

One of the earliest systems of using visual memory aids is believed to have been invented by the Greek orator Simonides of Ceos. Simonides was among the most respected orators of his time. He relied on strong mental images, coupled with associations he was familiar with (such as a well-known location), to fix information in his mind. We must remember that having a good memory was an admired skill in ancient Greece.

During the 3rd Century, the respected thinker Porphyry of Tyros is known to have created the earliest types of Mind Maps to represent graphically Aristotle's concept categories. Another person who used this concept before Buzan was the Majorcan writer and philosopher Ramon Lull.

The father of modern Mind Maps, however, is considered to be Dr. Allan Collins. He tapped into the use of the semantic network as a theory to explain how humans learn and eventually developed this theory into the concept of Mind Mapping. Collins' dedication and published research (as well as his efforts to understand the relationship between learning, creativity, and graphical thinking) in the early 1960s earned him that coveted title. Another respected researcher during that period, M. Ross Quillian, also contributed to its development.

More recently, Tony Buzan, a popular author in the field of education and learning, has taken the concept of Mind Maps and improved it. He has a website where one can find books and training to learn about the subject, as well as software to help anyone make them.

CHAPTER ONE - ADVANTAGES AND DISADVANTAGES OF MIND MAPS

Advantages

More Compatible with the Brain

Mind Maps are an effective way to improve learning and memorization because they are more compatible with the way the brain functions. Rather than the linear mode of note-taking, Mind Maps resemble the brain's neurological structure. This structure functions by linking thousands of little protrusions on the *arms* of a brain cell with the protrusions of other brain cells. In fact, one human brain can have an incalculable number of inter-neural links and pathways.

To make this concept clear, our brains are composed of billions and billions of neurons as illustrated in the picture below. A neuron represents the core component of the brain.

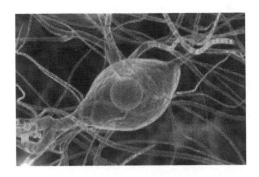

Within each neuron stems hundreds to sometimes thousands of branch-like connections called *dendrites*. These dendrites or links connect to other neurons (as shown below), and together they make up the complex structure of the brain.

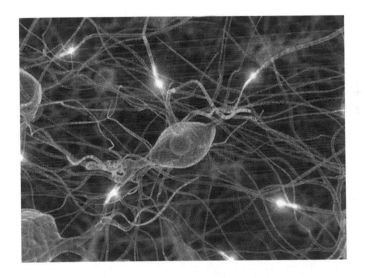

Mind Maps are structured the same way. Looking down at the diagram we showed earlier, we see that Mind Maps work in accordance with how our brain processes information. One idea is interconnected to many other ideas. This helps us understand, relate, and connect information so we can process and memorize it quicker, faster, and better.

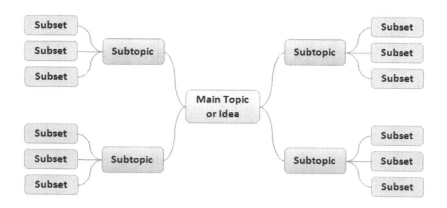

Balances the Brain

Another advantage of Mind Mapping is that it trains both hemispheres of the brain to be balanced and active at the same time. Our brains are divided into two hemispheres, the left and right. In most people, the right part of our brain is tasked with visual, associative, and non-verbal thinking as well as a lot of creative thinking. The left hemisphere, on the other hand, is responsible for analytical thoughts, which can be examined only one at a time—such as when we are writing. Studies have shown that drawing in the less-used hemisphere (usually the right) and using it in tandem with the dominant hemisphere produces a significant increase in the individual's total abilities and effectiveness.

This happens because multiple sensory channels are employed at the same time, allowing multiple intelligences to be drawn together. Usually, we find it difficult to express our thoughts on paper. However, when the right hemisphere is triggered in tandem with the left hemisphere, such as when we are producing a Mind Map, we overcome this difficulty. Surprisingly, when both hemispheres are stimulated in this way, the result is performance that is not just twice, but rather five to ten times more effective.

Emphasizes Associations

Association, in this context, means that you remember better those things which are interrelated compared to those which are not connected in any way. You can prove this to yourself: How many times does the right idea crop up in your mind? Doesn't it usually pop up when you bump into something that is related to that concept?

For example, you could be trying to remember where you placed your car keys– you just know you had them with you when you parked the car last night. So you look on the dining table to see where your keys are. The dining table reminds you that you had an after-dinner snack last night and that you went into the kitchen to prepare the snack. Suddenly you remember—your car keys are next to the microwave. You put them there when you were warming up your food. You always knew where the keys were; you just had to make the right link so you could remember.

Association is valuable for comprehension and understanding, particularly when used in taking notes and mapping out your study activities. You can improve your learning if you deliberately search for ways that different topics are interrelated.

With Mind Maps you do that. The technique was developed based on the human mind's special way of relating thoughts to each other. You take ideas and figure out how they connect to one another. That is how you create branches and set the various hierarchies. By taking the time to do this, you are able to understand and remember the information better.

A linear way of note-taking, according to Tony Buzan, actually limits creativity and memory since there is little leeway for the brain to create associations about ideas. In addition, using line-by-line or list-style notes trains the brain to think that there is a limit to the links between ideas—once the reader comes to the end of the list, he has finished. In reality, links between ideas go on infinitely in our minds.

Uses Keywords

The other aspect of Radiant Thinking is its use of keywords connected to the central main idea. A keyword is simply a word that summarizes an idea. For example, if you were to Mind Map this book, the main idea could be represented by the keyword *Mind Map* and would be placed in the center of the diagram. A keyword for one of the supporting ideas could be *Advantages*, as it corresponds to a subtopic that is discussed within these pages.

Research headed by Dr. Gordon Howe of Exeter University shows that note-taking improves when there are keywords, and the shorter the keyword, the better it is for retention of information. The reason is that relying on keywords during note-taking reduces the amount of unnecessary notes by 90%. Out of the plethora of words which we see, speak, and hear, most of that information can be summarized with keywords, which make up just 1% to 10% of that total. This boosts your effective writing/note-taking speed by up to 10 times.

Simplifies Complicated Information

Mind Maps work well when one is dealing with a complex scenario, particularly those which require a bird's eye view if they are to be understood. That's because the system structures information in relation to other data, which helps to identify which concepts are more important than others, which concepts are subsets of others, and which concepts are totally unrelated. To illustrate, let's take a look at this Mind Map again.

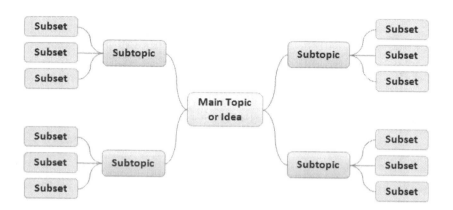

Looking at the diagram, you can see that the keyword in the center is important because it is the main idea. We can also see that the subtopics support the main topic and the subsets support the subtopic. Not only that, but we can easily see any of the subsets of the subtopic on the top left are unrelated to ideas in the top right, bottom right, or bottom left.

This is useful when you have muddled thoughts that need to be sorted out or bits and pieces of information whose relationships to one another have to be visualized. When you use Mind Maps this way, complex problems become simpler to think through and easier to find solutions for.

Enhances Creativity

Mind Mapping helps one become more creative as it emphasizes brainstorming, free association, and radiant thinking. That's because your level of comprehension of ideas is graphically represented, which then translates to a higher level of understanding when extended to other ideas or subtopics. Also, words are representations of ideas in your head, so every word is linked to an idea, which in turn is connected to a lot of other ideas stored in your brain. Since every word you can think of can trigger a host of associations in your mind, creativity is encouraged. This helps you see different and creative ways that ideas are related to one another. If you are persistent enough, you may be able to come up with a unique combination of relationships between ideas that may translate into a new product or service.

Makes It Faster to Take and Review Notes

Mind Maps speed up the process of taking notes because drawing your ideas in the form of keywords or symbols is a quicker process than laboriously writing down rows of notes. That is, instead of using long sentences to explain the relationship between a main topic to its subtopics or subtopics to its subsets, you make the connections simply by using lines and arrows. This saves a lot of writing time.

Mind Maps speed up the process to review notes because they take advantage of the human mind's ability to see an image as a whole instead of in isolated parts. When you look at a friend's face, your eyes and mind process the face as a whole to recognize the person. You do not look at the eyes, nose, mouth, wrinkles, and every bit of information separately to identify a friend. This is the theory behind Mind Maps. With them, you are able to view the entire series of relationships between ideas with just one look.

This means that instead of reading each piece of information and then reading how each piece is related or connected to others, you simply look at the map and your brain automatically sees the relationships. This eases the cognitive load on your mind and enables you to have a quick overview of the subjects you are noting.

Employs Spatial Mnemonics

Mind Maps also function as a spatial structure mnemonics. Your mind can trigger memories of things based on where it is placed. If you can remember where one idea is located, you will be able to recall other ideas around it. The location of one idea acts as a visual cue that triggers memory of other ideas. That is, by recalling the placement of a branch on your map, you will trigger memory of the ideas around that branch, and those ideas will trigger memory of concepts around them, and on and on. This is how spatial mnemonics work. By remembering where something is located, you trigger the recollection of other items around it.

Disadvantages

Requires Habit Change

Although Mind Maps have many advantages, they also have some drawbacks. For starters, they require that you change your habit of linear thinking. As studies show, it's not easy to change old ways of doing things, especially changing from the linear system that we have been taught to use since childhood to a very different way of writing down notes. However, all worthwhile progress requires change.

Requires Getting Used to

In addition, when you approach a new subject, you may not have a clear enough grasp of it to be able to organize your thoughts about it from the start. To make a good Mind Map, you need to choose your main subject, the subsidiary ideas around it, and the appropriate keywords. If you do not have all the information, you might not have sufficient information to choose the ideas and keywords. For this situation, linear note-taking might be more appropriate in the beginning. Once you get a better grasp of the subject, you can convert it into a Mind Map.

Furthermore, when you Mind Map, everything is supposed to be contained on a single page, but you don't necessarily know where a subject is going to take you and how much space should be allotted to a particular sub-group. It can be irritating when you want to add something to a category and there isn't enough room in that part of the page. This is another, yet minor, drawback of the technique.

Conflicts with Spoken Language

Lastly, even though Mind Mapping is said to be more intuitive than linear note-taking, this assumption is not entirely true. Language is first and foremost auditory, and writing is translating the auditory messages into a more permanent form. Speaking is principally linear, and the linear writing method is the one that comes closest to our way of speaking.

These are the advantages and disadvantages to using Mind Maps. For the most part, the positives outweigh the negatives if you are willing to take the time to learn this new and dynamic method of note taking. If you are willing, keep reading.

CHAPTER TWO - HOW TO MAKE A MIND MAP

Here is how you would create your own personal Mind Map. Simply put, first you draw an image of your central main idea in the middle of a blank piece of paper. From the central main idea, you radially link supporting ideas around it. Then, to the supporting ideas, you link ideas that are subsets of those. This is the fundamental process of Mind Mapping.

Use keywords for your central main idea and the supporting ideas. As mentioned earlier, keywords are easier to remember than whole sentences (which is why Mind Maps are superior to linear note-taking). Good keywords are those that describe or hone in on the topic or idea the best.

You may use various polygons of any sort (not just square) drawn around the main topic and then the subtopics to set them apart from one another. You could also try numbering each branch to show order or sequence.

Lines radiating from the central main idea ought to be thicker, while lines flowing from a supporting idea to its subset can be thinner. Each line should allow enough space to print the supporting idea allocated for that space.

Remember that there is essentially no limit to how vast your Mind Map can become. A subtopic in the first Mind Map you create may become the central key idea in the next one you draw. Each subtopic in a map is in effect the center of another map. This is the beauty of the technique—relationships may go on as extensively as they exist in your mind.

It is possible that in the course of drawing your Mind Map, you may have repeated a keyword twice or several times. Examine this closely. Decide whether the keyword warrants having its own branch or being a central idea for its own Mind Map. It is possible that the keyword may generate a whole host of related ideas which can be organized in a unique branch or map. If you are using this technique to brainstorm solutions to a problem, repeating a keyword is a positive sign—it could mean that you have discovered a potential solution or a key ingredient to a potential solution.

During the course of drawing your Mind Map, it is possible that you will not know all the subtopics and their subsets right away. That's o.k.—just add some lines that do not contain any information at all. You could take a break during this time, perhaps do something else for a while, and then come back to the task again. You may find that new associations grow in your mind when you do this. As the new associations grow, jot them in the blank lines.

By the way, there is no such thing as a stupid idea when you are free-associating. An idea that seems inane or dumb when you first think of it may be a truly creative, great concept when you examine it later.

Another thing that may happen is that you could think of a really fantastic idea at inopportune times (for instance, when you're taking a shower or driving your car). It helps to have a notepad in order to jot down such ideas and then transfer them to your Mind Map later on. Why this happens is because your unconscious was still thinking of your Mind Map even when you were doing something else—then it came up with that association which you simply had to write down. If paper is not at hand, try to keep that ground-breaking thought in your mind until you can get to your diagram. You really need to put down your brainchild on paper, though—think of it as a brain purge. Otherwise, your conscious will nag you that you have thoughts which need to be jotted.

Example

To illustrate how one would do a Mind Map, below we've put together a Mind Map of this book.

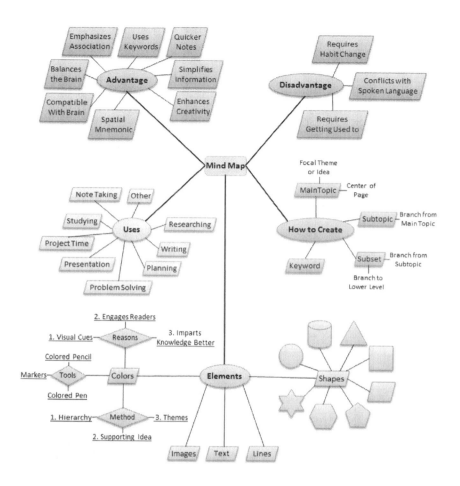

As you can see, you start out in the center with the main topic. The main idea of this book is Mind Maps. From here, you draw out lines to the supporting ideas. Within each supporting idea, you draw out more lines which detail the important points of that idea.

If you notice, we are able to summarize a large part of this book in considerable detail and clarity in a single page. At a quick glance, you can see that this book talks about the seven advantages and three disadvantages of using Mind Maps, how to create them, and different areas where one can apply the technique. This book also discusses its five elements: *colors*, *shapes*, *lines*, *images*, and *text*. It would take you couple of pages of written notes and considerably more time to get the same information you did here with a quick glance.

Also notice our use of polygons to distinguish the various hierarchical levels. For the main topic, we use a square; for the subtopic we use circles; within the subtopic we use trapezoids, and within them we use diamonds. This helps to organize the information visually because anytime you see a circle, you automatically know that thought supports the main idea, and anytime you see a trapezoid, you know it is a subset of the supporting idea. Using shapes to emphasize hierarchy in this way helps your mind to structure the information so you can understand it better. We will talk a little more about using shapes in the next chapter.

More importantly, pay attention to the use of colors. Observe how each subtopic and all its supporting ideas are highlighted with their own color. The subsequent chapter will go more into detail about the use of color as well, but notice how we use colors here to improve the overall clarity of the information. In this example, anytime you see keywords or ideas in green, you know these ideas all relate to the *Uses* of Mind Maps and are unrelated to other subtopics like *Advantages*, which are in blue.

For the sake of clarity, we did not go too deeply into this Mind Map. However, if you wanted, you could go further by adding more details or subsets to any of the supporting ideas. How far in depth you want to go is up to you.

Not only can you decide how much detail to add to your Mind Map, but you can also decide how to organize the topics and subtopics. For instance, you could easily organize the Mind Map by chapter. Instead of using the above subtopics, *Advantage, Disadvantage, Uses*, etc., your subtopics could be Chapter 1, Chapter 2, Chapter 3, and so on. All the supporting ideas would summarize the details discussed within each chapter. The attractiveness of Mind Maps is that you can organize information whichever way helps you understand it best.

CHAPTER THREE – ELEMENTS OF A MIND MAP

Color

Before starting the discussion on color, it's important to point out that in this book we refer to quite a number of Mind Map diagrams. Unfortunately, these diagrams are not in color, rather black and white. Since this book is independently published, printing it in color would nearly triple its purchase price. In order to keep the print edition price of this book affordable for readers, we opted to go this route. Nevertheless, this will not affect your understanding of the material because we will explain the inner-workings of each Mind Map in detail. This way you can still grasp the important concepts of color and how to properly apply it. Let's proceed.

When you communicate, only 7% of the meaning is conveyed to the brain through words. Your mind relies more on visual cues. Thus visual elements like shape and color enhance the process of communication.

Line-by-line note-taking usually relies on only two colors—black (the color of your pen) and white (the color of your paper). The use of these two colors in combination has a hypnotic effect on the viewer, which may explain why so many people fall asleep reading or are lulled into a trance-like state in a classroom.

The writer Ronald E. Green, in *The Persuasive Properties of Color*, revealed that colorful visual aids make readers more eager to read and willing to participate by an amazing 80%. Companies that stress color as a key feature in their products really understand that not only can they sell their products better, but color really works at imparting knowledge better as well. Jan V. White of *Color for Impact* noted that presentations which incorporate color are actually 60% more simple to view. In addition, such presentations cut down on search time by 80%, boost attention span by 82%, and enhance comprehension by 70%. White further stressed that color in presentations improves recall by 60% and brand recognition by 70%.

If you have ever looked at the weather map in the newspaper or on the evening news, you will notice that it is colored in different parts to show the differences in the weather in various parts of the country. These maps are easier to look at and understand than a black and white map. Not only that, these maps are much quicker to process than reading a text that sets out to explain the weather. This is an application of the same principle in Mind Mapping: color is the lifeblood of visual aids.

Color coding when Mind Mapping can be done in different ways: by hierarchy, by subtopic, by themes or any other way that seems right for you. Color coding by theme acts like a traffic sign informing you what that part of your Mind Map is generally about. Color coding by subtopic (as shown by the example in the previous chapter) denotes that all subsets of ideas belong to a specific subtopic. Color by hierarchy separates the main idea, supporting idea, and their subsets from each other.

Below is an example of how a Mind Map would look if you color coded it by hierarchy. It is the same map from the previous chapter, except that the colors have been changed.

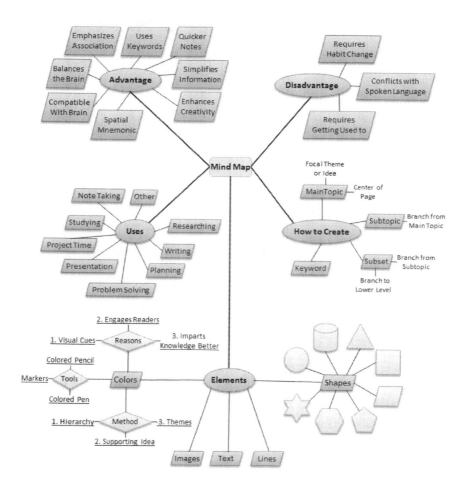

In this illustration, the main branches are in blue, the sub-branches are in pink, and the subsets are in a light green. Again, it is the same map, but highlighted to emphasize hierarchy. This is an effective way to arrange colors because any time you see a keyword in blue, you quickly know it is a subtopic. If you see an idea or thought highlighted in pink, you know it is a subset of a subtopic. Using colors like this makes the hierarchy more apparent.

Color coding becomes easier if you have the right tools. Effective tools include colored pens, highlighters, and colored pencils (though these may provide less clarity). Some people prefer to sketch their Mind Maps with pencil first, then color in the appropriate areas later on. Doing this makes it easier to change, modify, or erase an idea or branch before finalizing the map.

Polygons

In the previous chapter, we pointed out one approach to using polygons to organize your Mind Map. Now, you do not have to order the polygons this way. You can use circles first or diamonds first. It is really a matter of preference.

Another option is not to vary the use of polygons. That is, you might choose to create Mind Maps that use only circles or only squares. Shapes, like colors, are useful for visually spacing out like ideas from unlike ideas. However, variations in shapes can sometimes be distracting. If the use of multiple polygons confuses or distracts you, stick to using a uniform shape in your Mind Map.

If you do decide to vary the polygons, however, you can apply them like color. You can use polygons to differentiate hierarchy, as in the examples above. You can use polygons by topic, applying a unique shape for each main branch. Or you can apply polygons by theme. As with color, polygons give you assorted ways to organize content.

Lines

Another element to consider when creating a Mind Map is the appearance of lines. When we say lines, we mean the branches that connect one topic to another. As mentioned earlier, you can alter lines by adding thickness. That is, lines that branch from the main topic would be thicker than the lines that branch from the subtopics. Consequently, the lines that branch from the subsets would be thinner.

If you use lines this way, you do not necessarily have to add polygons at the end of them. The variation in thickness will indicate the hierarchy. Therefore, instead of placing a keyword or idea within a circle or square, you can place it on the branch itself. This is useful because concepts of longer length don't have to be squeezed within the confines of a restricted shape. Here is an example of a Mind Map focusing entirely on lines.

As you can see above, this map does not use polygons of any sort. Like a tree, it uses thick lines branching out from the center, with thinner lines branching out from main branches and even thinner lines branching out from the sub-branches. As mentioned, since there are no shapes being used, the content is written directly on the branch. Even more, with no shapes to color, variations in color are applied to the lines themselves. It is the same map with the same content, but displayed differently. This is another approach to organizing your Mind Map.

Images

The next element to consider is image. In the sample Mind Maps above, under the topic of Polygon, we didn't write out the specific shapes that one could use. We didn't write *square*, *triangle*, *circle*, etc. In place of these words; we put in a corresponding picture. This is an example of using images.

Since this is a visual technique, it helps to incorporate images or other visual cues within your map when possible. As you learned earlier, your mind processes images more quickly and understands them better than text. When you see images, there is no word or sentence you need to read or comprehend. Your mind quickly takes in and makes sense of the information.

Other ways we could use images may include replacing the keywords *Advantage* and *Disadvantage* with a thumbs up and thumbs down icon. Or under the topic *Tools*, we could replace the words *colored pencil*, *colored pen*, and *marker* with images of such items. This would help you to better remember and recall the information.

Be cautious, though, of how you employ images. While images are quicker to process and easier to remember, they present some drawbacks. Often, images are not as concrete as words. For example, a thumbs up icon may not necessarily imply the word *Advantage*. It could just as well imply the words *approved*, or for a Facebook user, *like*. To someone else, it could mean something different; therefore, be careful how you feature images.

Text

The most important element in a mind map is text. This is obvious because without it, your diagram would simply be a collection of colored lines attached to shapes and images. In some types of maps, like those for children, this might prove useful. Majority of them, though, are going to employ text. Since text is essential to the system, there are a couple of ways you can vary it to make your Mind Maps more visual, and hence, easier to read and use.

One way is to vary the capitalization of words. For the main topic you might put the text in all caps, the subtopic with just the first letter of each word in caps, and the subsets in lower case. This helps define or establish hierarchy. If your Mind Map gets messy, seeing the words in all caps will make the main topic stand out from the rest of the text.

Another thing you can do is apply formatting like bold and italics. You can do it to define hierarchy or simply to highlight a specific word. If you want to define hierarchy, you can put the main topic in bold, the subtopics in italics, and not apply formatting to the lower-level topics. Otherwise you can use bold or italics as a way to stress the importance of the word.

Lastly, you can apply a numbering system. If the branches on your map discuss steps or have a specific sequence, you can number each branch to make the sequence apparent. Even more, you can use Roman numerals to make the hierarchy clear. You can use I, II, III, IV for the first level branches, A, B, C, D, for the second level branches, i, ii, iii, iv for the third level, and so on. This is essentially a practice used in outlines, but by incorporating it into a Mind Map, you get the best of both worlds.

Which Elements to Use and When

Above we discussed the five elements of a Mind Map— color, polygon, line, image, and text. It is important to recognize that each element has its shortcoming. The shortcoming of color is that you have to carry around various types of colored instruments. The issue with creating lines of varying thickness is that it takes time to fill in those lines. The problem with images is that creating drawings by hand is not only time consuming, but requires a certain level of skill. The drawback to text is that it is does not stand out as well as color or shapes.

As a result, how you employ each element depends on what you are Mind Mapping and where. If you are taking notes of a lecture, you will not have a lot of time to switch between numerous colored pens nor time to shade in lines of varying degrees of thickness. In these instances, polygons become useful. With polygons, you can quickly draw shapes around a keyword or set of keywords to differentiate topics or to establish hierarchy. On the other hand, if you are at home summarizing a book, you will have more time to color and shade.

If you are creating Mind Maps using computer software, many of the limitations the use of colors and images present are done away with. With software, you can apply colors at will, add thickness to branches, and grab images from the internet while quickly and easily incorporating them into your map. However, the problem with software is that you need to be in front of a computer. That may prove difficult if you are in a presentation, meeting, or a lecture. Furthermore, most software has restrictions on the control and appearance of hierarchies. The more you get into using this system, the more you will figure out what works with your needs and the needs of the situation.

Now that you have a comprehensive introduction to Mind Mapping and are aware of its important elements, let's look at ways to apply the technique. In the subsequent chapters, we will show you how to use it for note taking, brainstorming, planning, and more. As we present the instructions, we will also provide illustrations. We will vary these illustrations to incorporate the above-mentioned elements as much as possible so you can become accustomed to the different ways Mind Maps can be put together. Let's proceed.

CHAPTER FOUR – TAKING NOTES WITH MIND MAPS

Note taking is an important activity, particularly for students and professionals. Mind Maps were initially created to aid learners who take down notes, so it is especially useful in this area. It can help you take better notes with less effort. In this chapter you will learn to take notes of books and lectures.

Books

People take notes of books for several reasons. Some take notes to remember the important details for an exam or to create an overview for a report, while others do it to gather research. In this section, we will show you how to use Mind Maps in these three tasks.

Taking Notes of Books

To take notes of books using Mind Maps, start by browsing the book. Browsing means skimming through its various sections and familiarizing yourself with the content. Browsing is important because it gives you a better feel for what will be discussed and how the information will be laid out. This helps you more easily understand the key points and the relationships between those points. This will make it quicker to set up the branches and hierarchy in your map.

How much material you browse will depend on how much of the book you are going to or are required to read and learn. If you are reading a textbook for class, you will likely be reading one chapter or section at a time, so you will browse only that chapter or section. On the other hand, if you are reading a traditional book like a "how to" guide or manual, you will need to read it cover to cover, thus requiring that you first browse it cover to cover.

To browse a chapter or section, read the chapter headings, summaries, words in bold, underline, and italics, as well as illustrations and end of chapter notes and questions if there happen to be any. To browse an entire book, read the front and back of the book, go through the table of contents and other indexes, read the introduction and concluding chapters, and skim through the interior chapters. As you skim through the interior chapters, again pay attention to items in bold, underline, and italics as well as any illustrations and end of chapter notes and questions.

If you are Mind Mapping an entire book, it is recommended that you still focus on one chapter or section at a time. Some books are too big or contain too many critical details to fit in a single map. Unless you are looking for a general overview or summary, which we will discuss in the next section, you will want to break up your reading, and hence, your Mind Mapping of the material. You can divide the reading by chapter, groups of related chapters, or if the chapters are lengthy, smaller sections or subsections of a chapter. Nonetheless, whether you take notes one book at a time or one section at a time, make sure to browse the material to get a better awareness of what it is about and the main points in it.

After you develop a general understanding of the material and how it is structured, you can begin reading. While reading, pay close attention to the main ideas and keywords. It helps not to try to Mind Map while you read, but instead just read it straight through. Trying to Mind Map while you read will disrupt the flow of reading and make it difficult for your mind to make important associations between concepts, especially if those associations appear in the later parts of the text.

After you finish reading, you can begin drawing your map. For the main idea, put both the title of the book or chapter and the keyword that best sums up its idea. This way you know at a glance what chapter the notes came from and what it is about. You may also find it helpful to write down on which page the chapter starts.

Now, create subtopics for the most important ideas that are discussed. These will be the general concepts the author spends time talking about. In some books each key idea will have a subheading. For example, in Chapter 1 of this book we have the key ideas of *advantages* and *disadvantages* under their respective subheadings. If you want, you can use these subheadings to define the subtopics. However, don't worry if your subtopics don't exactly line up with the way the book is set up. The important thing is to identify the essential points of the text.

Once you identify the subtopics, begin adding subsets using important facts and noteworthy details about that subtopic. Do this by first jotting down anything that sticks out in your mind. Don't worry if you can't recall everything; just note the pieces you do remember. Then go through the text again, pulling out other important ideas, concepts and facts. Record them within the appropriate branch or sub-branches.

Not every fact in a book will necessarily be important. If you are studying British history, the birth of William of Normandy probably isn't important, but the date he won the Battle of Hastings is. On the other hand, if you are studying William of Normandy, his birthday probably is important. Keep this in mind as you pick out the noteworthy points.

When you are done, everything that you want to remember from the book or chapter will be on your map. Follow these steps for the subsequent chapters, keeping all of them together in a folder or notebook so they don't get lost. When you are done, you'll have Mind Maps for the entire book, with all the important points and ideas. It's good practice to label each map with the title and author of the book, so that if one of the maps gets separated, you'll know where to put it back.

For an example of how this might come together, you can explore any of the mind maps presented above. They illuminate how to note books using this technique. This book is not terribly long, so we are able to summarize it within one Mind Map. If we wanted, we could delve deeper by adding additional subtopics and subsets or expanding each subtopic or subset into its own Mind Map. For more content-heavy books, you may opt to create several Mind Maps to cover all the necessary details you want to learn and remember.

Creating an Overview of a Book

Sometimes a person is not required to know the details of a book, but rather generate an overview. Students writing a report, a review, or recommending a specific book to be used for a course study or project can use Mind Maps to organize their thoughts into an overview. They can then reference the map while writing their report or review.

Making a Mind Map for a book report or review is different from making it for note taking. When you take notes from a book, you are gathering noteworthy facts and data. When you prepare for a review or report, you want to record a general overview of what the book is about and your reactions to the content. Usually the information you need for a review or book report can easily fit in a single Mind Map.

The first step to making an overview Mind Map is to decide what subtopics to use. This seems out of order, but there is a reason for it. Your main topic is easy—the *title* of the book. You can write that down right away. Your subtopics, on the other hand, can vary, and which you choose will determine how your overview is organized. Basically, the subtopics you pick will define how you will tackle the book.

As an example, for a novel, you might use subtopics of *Plot*, *Characters*, *Setting* and *Theme*. By using these as subtopics, you are organizing your thoughts and overview based on the literary devices that make up the book. If you are creating an overview of a non-fiction work, you might use the book's subheadings. For instance, a book on weight loss might break down the book by *diet*, *exercise*, and *motivation*, so you would use these as your subtopics. In general, you want your subtopics to be broad enough so that you can fit even the most isolated thought or idea somewhere. This involves picking subtopics that are distinct from each other, as to cover every basis.

After establishing the subtopic, you go further down and fill in the subsets for those subtopics. For a novel, that may include a discussion of the different characters, the themes in the story, etc. For non-fiction, that may involve listing facts, data, research, and any other information that supports the subtopic as well as your reactions to the information.

After going through all the subsets, you will have a solid overview of the book. This overview will include everything you need to write your report or review. The subtopics of your Mind Map will represent the sections or points of your writing. The subsets you wrote down will provide the details needed to flesh out each section and point to support your position. Altogether, a complete overview Mind Map can be a strong tool for creating a book report, review, or recommendation.

To illustrate how this will look, we will do an overview of the novel *To Kill a Mockingbird* by Harper Lee. The story in this novel takes place in the Deep South of the early 1930s. Even though slavery has been abolished for many years, many residents of Maycomb, Alabama, a fictional county, still carry a supremacist attitude. The story follows a brother and sister's day-to-day life as they come to grips with the snobbery and dark side of human nature during which time their father, the most respected lawyer in the county, takes on a case involving a black man accused of a crime he did not commit.

As stated earlier, when creating an overview, you start by determining what to include for subtopics. Since this is a work of fiction, we will summarize under the subtopics of main characters, theme, plot, setting, and key facts. Again, this example will be an overview. If you plan on delving deeper into the book, it is advised that you follow the instructions above in the section on *Taking Notes of Books Using Mind Maps* and create a separate diagram for each area or chapter requiring analysis. We start as shown below.

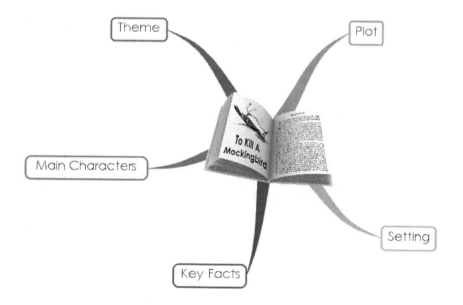

As you see, we placed the title of the book in the center, as this is the main topic of the map. Around the main topic, we placed main characters, theme, plot, setting, and key facts, the subtopics by which we decided to organize the content. When doing this for your own overview, be sure to lay out the branches evenly and in a way where you can add more information to those branches that require additional detail. Here we know that the *main characters* branch will be more involved than the *theme* or *key facts*, so we spaced them accordingly.

Next we fill in the subtopics with their subsets. In this example, we start with the characters. This story has quite a few characters. Some of the main ones include Tom Robinson, the defendant; Atticus Finch, the defending attorney; and Mayella Ewell, the plaintiff. We add them and others to the map by extending sub-branches as illustrated below.

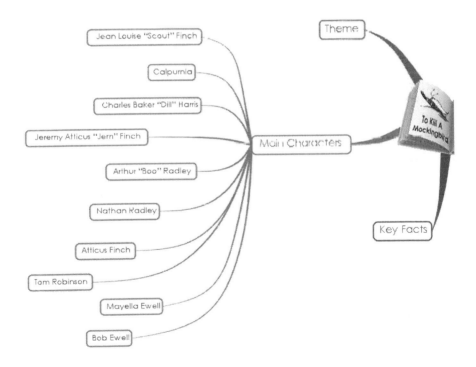

Working in a clockwise motion (although this is not a requirement), we move onto populating the *themes* branch of the Mind Map. Using the same color as that of the main branch, we extend sub-branches while listing the different themes found in the novel. Although there are numerous themes in this book, we listed the prevalent ones—good vs. evil, social inequality, and importance of moral education. You can see this in the diagram below.

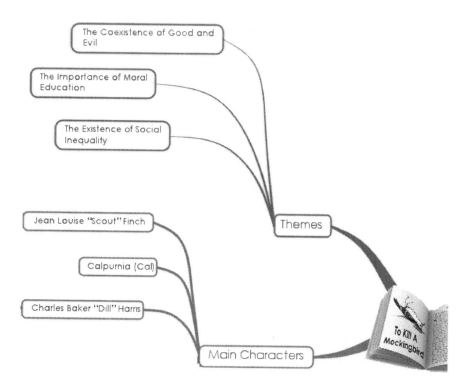

From here, we continue moving clockwise to populate the remaining subtopics. As addressed earlier, the *plot* revolves around the accusation of a man for a crime he did not commit. The *key facts* relating to the novel depend on what information you are expected or need to know and remember. In our example, we covered only the author's name, the type of literary work, its genre, the language of the piece and its point of view. Again we apply all the previously discussed features to make for bright and appealing graphics that are easy to review and remember later on.

Now the last subtopic—setting. Here we add in the fictional county of Maycomb and the state in which it is located, Alabama. We also mention the year the story takes place and expand it to show that it occurred during the Great Depression. We add another image, using dynamic colors and clear text to ensure that the information is presented well. The map below displays these details.

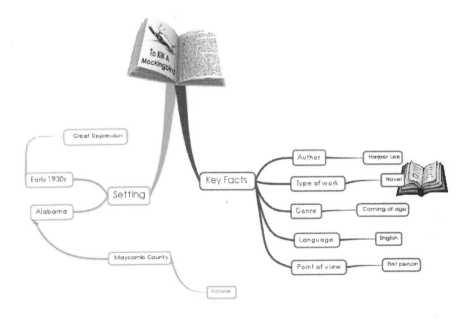

After doing all this, we have a Mind Map that gives us an informative overview of the book. We have all the characters laid out so we know who is involved. We have the setting establishing where and when the story takes place. More importantly, we have the fine points of the theme, plot, and key facts—everything needed to overview this book.

At this point, if we wanted, we could go further by expanding on the subsets. For example, our summary of the characters is very vague. We listed only their names, but nothing else. It would also help to include their descriptions, the role they play in the story, as well their relationship to one another. This is the nice thing about Mind Maps: We can expand on subtopics and subsets as much as we want or need to comprehend a topic fully. The illustration below shows us delving deeper into the *characters* branch.

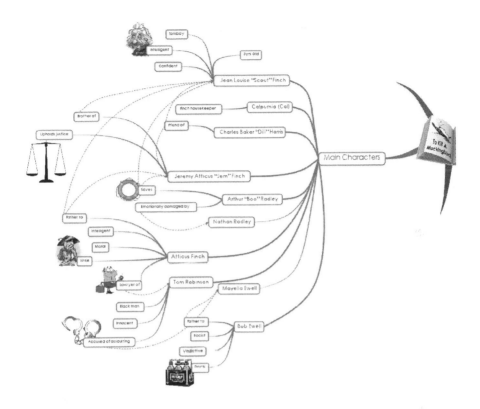

Looking above, you can see how much more we have for each character. We even have dotted lines that establish relationships like the one that goes from Atticus Finch, the father, to Jean Louise Finch, the daughter. We've even incorporated images to connect the descriptions to specific characters more memorably.

So that covers using a Mind Map to create an overview of a book. The last topic in this section discusses how to use it for research.

Performing Research from Books

Sometimes you need information from more than just one book. That is, you need to combine information from several books. This type of note taking requires a different kind of Mind Map—a research Mind Map. A research Mind Map gathers notes from several places together in one place. This type of Mind Mapping also makes it possible to organize research by subject rather than source.

Research Mind Maps have several uses. They can be used to gather information for a report or research paper. Someone preparing a presentation or proposal might create a research map to gather evidence supporting his or her position. A Mind Map like this can even be used to organize information for a business plan or grant proposal.

Before beginning your research Mind Map, you need to decide what topic you will be researching and what information you want to gather. Someone preparing to open a business might research the local market, demographics and competition. A student writing a paper on the author Robert Louis Stevenson might want to find out about his life, the culture he lived in, his writing and his legacy. Only you can know what information you will need for your project.

If you don't know much about the subject you are researching, it might help to do some preliminary investigation before making any decisions. You can do this by picking up some introductory books on the subject and scanning through them. Don't worry about taking notes at this point. You're just trying to get a general idea about your topic. Essentially, you are *browsing* about the topic. By educating yourself through the browse step, you will be able to determine what types of information you need to gather in your research.

Once you have determined what types of information you need for your research, you can start the Mind Map. The main topic will be the subject you are researching. The subtopics will be the different aspects of the subject for which you are seeking information or answers. Don't put any subsets down just yet—this is what you are trying to collect from the research.

From here, you will gather research material. These would be the books that contain the relevant information. You can gather relevant information from other avenues as well—the internet, newspapers, even interviews and observation. However, for the discussion and examples here, we'll focus on books. If you don't have the books you need at home, you can find good research material on many topics at your local library or a local university library. Try to gather at least three sources of information—this way if controversy or disagreements exist, you are likely to see several sides of the issue.

Before beginning your research, it helps to create a *research key*. A research key helps you keep track of which source your information came from. You may decide to use a different color pen for each source, or refer to one book as *book A*, another book as *book B* and so on. Whatever system you choose, write down the title and author of each book and what its code is on the side of the Mind Map.

Pick one book to start with, sit down with your Mind Map, and start reading. Feel free to skip chapters of the book that are irrelevant to your research. It is up to you whether you make notes as you go or read the relevant chapters straight through first before writing down the notes. Remember that for some types of research, you will need to note down the page number from where you are taking information for later reference.

Once you add the relevant information from a book to your Mind Map, add a code to all the branch and sub-branches so you know from which book the information came. Then pick up the next book and read through it the same way you read through the first one. As you read, fill in your map with the appropriate detail. When you are done going through all your research materials, read over your Mind Map to ensure it is complete.

Often when doing a research Mind Map, your map will not be complete the first time through. Instead, the research materials will be short on some of the information you need. Sometimes it can help to read through your research materials again to make sure you didn't miss important points. Otherwise, head back to the library and see what other research materials you can find that you didn't grab the first time. It may take three or even four sets of research materials before you are satisfied with the amount and detail of the information that you have.

To see how this might work, let's take a look at Dennis, a student doing research on Japanese history. He needs to gather information on the history of Japan until World War I for a school paper. He is somewhat familiar with Japanese history from his classes and decides he needs more information on four major periods of Japanese history: the Heian period, the Muramachi period, the Tokugawa era, and the Meiji Restoration. The main topic of his Mind Map is *Japanese History through WWI*. The subtopics are the four periods of Japanese history on which he wants to gather information.

Dennis is able to use his school textbook for some of his research, but he needs more in-depth information. He goes to the university library and borrows three books on the history of Japan and one on the history of Asia. He is not allowed to use the internet because his teacher does not consider it a reliable source of information. With the four books from the library and his text books, he has his research materials and is almost ready to begin. Before he begins reading, he decides he will use a different color for each book. He writes down which color will be for which book, starting with a black pen for his text book.

Sitting down with his textbook, some colored pens and his Mind Map, Dennis begins reading. He doesn't read the whole book in detail; instead he skips whole chapters that have nothing to do with his research. Focusing on the chapters about Japanese history, he looks specifically for information about his four periods. When he gets to these chapters he reads them through, getting a general idea of the information they contain. Then he goes back and starts at the beginning of the chapter. This time as he reads, he stops to fill in his map as he finds information. He is able to write down that the Heian period was from 794-1185 CE, the Muromachi period is also called Ashikaga, and other relevant facts.

When he finishes getting information out of his textbook, Dennis makes sure that he has written down a page number next to each piece of information for the footnotes of his paper. Then he picks up one of the books on Japanese history and a blue pen. He reads through each book in the same way. At the end, he has all the information he could want about the Muromachi period, Tokugawa era and Meiji Restoration. Unfortunately, his sources didn't have much about the Heian period.

A trip back to the library doesn't help much as they don't have any more books on Japanese history. Dennis decides to ask the librarians for help. They are able to order several more books for him through interlibrary loan, including one specifically about the Heian period. Dennis continues his investigation and eventually fills his research Mind Map. From here, he has all the information he needs to start writing his paper.

For lengthier, more complex research, you may need to create multiple Mind Maps. What if Dennis had to do a paper of a longer length, such as a term paper? He wouldn't have been able to fit all the required information for a term paper on a single diagram. Instead, he would create a separate Mind Map for each period. He would create one for the Heian period, one for the Muromachi period, and so on. He would do preliminary research on each period to come up with good subtopics for each Mind Map.

Also, it is possible that for a term paper, because it is more involved, as he gathered information, each of those subtopics would become a starting place for a new Mind Map. Dennis would just keep expanding his information web with more and more detailed Mind Maps until he had all the information he needed. This is how to vary the technique with more complex research.

These are the different ways to apply Mind Maps with written materials such as books. You can use them as a tool for note taking, a format for a book overview, or a way to organize research. No matter how you choose to use Mind Maps with books, they can make learning and absorbing information from the pages easier and more rewarding. Now that we are done looking at creating mind maps from books, let's look at speeches and lectures.

Speeches and Lectures

Attending speeches and lectures can be a great way to learn new information. However, it can be hard to remember everything afterward. Mind Maps can help you record and recall the information you hear in these types of settings. You can then study the information later and use it to organize a project or anything else. Having a Mind Map of the information can be a big help.

Making a Mind Map of a lecture or presentation is different from a book because you are making it in the moment. You won't be able to go back later and re-watch a lecture, the way you can re-read a book. This means you will need to be doing several things at once—listening to and watching the presenter, figuring out what the main ideas and subtopics are, drawing out the branches and catching the subsets that you want to record. But don't worry—it isn't as hard as it sounds.

Sometimes the presenter will help you out. He or she may hand out an outline of the presentation or begin the lecture with an overview of what will be covered. If the presenter does this, use it. The overview or outline can tell you what the main topic and subtopics of the presentation will be. Usually there will be a heading or title at the top. This heading tells you the main topic of the lecture. You can make this the main topic of your Mind Map.

As far as subtopics go, the ease of identifying them will depend on whether you are working from an outline or simply an overview. An outline will be divided into subsections. Each section will have a heading. These section headings will usually be the subtopics of the lecture and hence can be the subtopics of your Mind Map. An overview, on the other hand, may not have section headings sketched out as clearly. Instead, an overview will usually be divided into several paragraphs, with each paragraph summarizing a different part of the lecture. The summary in each paragraph can become a subtopic for your Mind Map.

During the presentation, the lecturer will address each subtopic in turn. As he does, listen for key ideas or important information you want to remember. Write these ideas down as subsets under the relevant subtopic. If the lecturer uses visual aids such as charts or diagrams, you can sketch a copy of these down as subsets as well.

If the lecturer does not give helpful starters like an outline or overview, you can still make an effective Mind Map of the lecture. In this case, the title of the lecture can still be the main topic; however, instead of gathering information from a handout to determine the subtopics, you will need to listen for them while the lecturer is speaking.

You will hear them at one of two places in the lecture. First, a lecturer may start off with a summary of his information. For instance, a speaker on the Vietnam War may start by saying "The discussion of today will be the cause, economic impact and opposition of the Vietnam War." In this case, the subtopics of the lecture (and your Mind Map) would be *Cause*, *Economic Impact*, and *Opposition*. You would write *Vietnam War* in the center, as that would be your main topic. Around the center you would have lines branching out to the subtopics *Cause*, *Economic Impact*, and *Opposition*.

The other place you can find subtopics in a lecture is at turning points. A turning point is where the lecture changes topics. There are several ways to recognize turning points in a lecture. If the speaker is using a slide show, there will often be a topic slide that has the title of the next section. If the speaker is not using a slide show, listen for turning phases. Turning phrases draw your attention to the new topic. Examples include "Now we are going to look at" or "Let's consider." Whatever topic the speaker mentions after a turning phrase is likely to be the next subtopic and hence a separate branch for your Mind Map.

Making the rest of the map is the same as if you have started from an overview or outline. Listen to the lecture and pay attention to any key points or important information. Write down the parts of the lecture you want to remember or feel are important as subsets. Don't forget to sketch out any interesting charts or visual aids.

Making a Mind Map from a lecture can be surprisingly easy, and the speaker works to make it that way. Remember, presenters and lecturers want you to take notes, so they try to organize their ideas by topic and will keep the relationship between different ideas clear. Most lectures will have cues to important information— anything from the classic *this will be on the test* to *you may find it interesting that . . . .* As you get to know individual lecturers, you can learn their cues and be alert to the important information before it comes.

And don't worry about needing to rush to get all the information down. Just as speakers organize their ideas to help with note taking in the audience, they also pace themselves. Many times a presenter will pause for a few moments to give listeners time to finish their notes on a key section. You don't have all the time in the world, but you should have enough time.

That about wraps up using Mind Maps to take notes. In the next chapter, we look at other uses of this technique.

CHAPTER FIVE – OTHER USES OF MIND MAPS

Note taking is one of the more common uses of Mind Maps, but there are many other applications of the tool. In this chapter, we will introduce you to those other applications, including studying, problem solving, presenting, and more. By the end, maybe you'll have some new uses of your own.

This chapter will introduce using Mind Maps for:

1. Studying

2. Writing

3. Brainstorming

4. Decision Making

5. Planning

6. Project Management

7. Estimating Project Time

8. Problem Solving

9. Diagnosis

10. Giving a Presentation

11. Recalling Information

12. Learning a Language

So let's get started.

Studying

Studying is one of the more popular applications of Mind Maps. Applying it for studying is closely related to applying it for note taking. You take notes using Mind Maps and then go over and review them to remember the material. You can study from Mind Maps you have made or maps that other people make.

The organization of a Mind Map helps to make studying easier. As you learned, the human mind remembers things better when it can understand connections between them. This makes the history of Europe or ocean ecology or any other subject a web of connected ideas to be understood, rather than a list of disconnected facts to be memorized. In this way, a Mind Map makes studying work in accordance with how your brain likes to learn and remember information.

The first step is obviously to create a Mind Map. This involves taking the information you want to learn or remember and bringing it together and organizing it into a Mind Map. You can include information from books, lecture, research or wherever else it resides.

The next step is to review it. Look at the layout of the map and determine where all the connections lie. Figure out why you broke out the subtopics the way you did. While reviewing information in the subset branches, make sure you know to which subtopic they belong. You can also read the information aloud to get the aural part of your brain involved in remembering. Finally, you can trace the branches with your finger, which engages the part of your mind that deals with kinesthesia. In all, you can use many different parts of your brain with a Mind Map, making it many times easier to retain the information.

After reviewing, test your knowledge of the information. First, put the map away so you can't see it. Then pick a piece of information and try to recall where it resides on the map. You may even try to recall the subtopic or higher level branches to which it is connected. The other thing you can do is pick a subtopic or subset and try to recall all the items within its lower levels. Then look at the illustration to see if you remembered the items correctly.

It also helps to visualize the map in your head. Close your eyes and imagine where the branches reside and the information contained in each branch. This way, when you are questioned or tested on the information, you can refer to the mental image to find the answer.

These are a few ways to study from Mind Maps. It is easiest to study from one that you have made because the organization and connections will always make sense to you. When you created it, you picked the subtopics that you saw as the crucial division of the main topics. As a result, the organization ends up being the same as the way your mind understood the ideas. This allows you to study and learn the information more easily.

You are not, however, limited to studying Mind Maps you've created. If you need to, you can also study maps made by someone else. If you use another person's map, you will need to learn the reason behind their organization. So before studying it, take a few moments to understand why that person organized the information the way he or she did. This will help you appreciate the associations their branches are built on. Once you understand the connections and associations, it will be easier to understand and remember the information. If their organization doesn't make sense to you when you read it, you can ask them to go over it with you and explain why they made those choices.

Writing

All of us have at one point or another been required to write. Writing is important because it helps assess how much you know about a subject and how well you can articulate that knowledge. However, not everyone can write well. Most people just compose sentence after sentence without any logic or order—then they wonder why people find what they have written difficult to read and understand.

Luckily you know about Mind Mapping. Whether you are writing a research paper, report, business plan or something else entirely, a Mind Map can help you organize your thoughts and plan your writing. Your writing will flow better, with every thought or idea clearly connected to other thoughts or ideas.

There are three main steps in writing. The first is to determine the premise. The premise is the central idea of your writing. It is the principal argument you are trying to make. If your writing is a punch, then the premise is your target. Everything you write is designed to reinforce this principal idea.

The second step is to develop the key points. The key points prove your premise. They provide evidence that your assertion is correct or give logical arguments to support it. If your premise is the target, then your key points are what you use to hit the target.

The third and last step is to review. Review allows you to see how precisely you hit your target. It helps ensure that your key points support the premise and that everything flows well from beginning to end. More importantly, it gives you a chance to catch problems in the initial draft so you can go back and resolve concerns.

Mind Maps aid in these three steps. They help you establish a premise, develop the points for the premise, and assist in the revision process. We go over each area in detail below.

Step 1. Determining a Premise

As you learned, a premise is the focal point of your paper. Having a clear premise is the most important part of the writing process. For example, if you were to write an essay about World War II, there are a lot of things you can discuss, everything from the political situation that led to the war to the Battle of Stalingrad to the home-front efforts of the US and British citizens. With all the possibilities, it would be very easy to write an essay that wanders all over the place without really saying anything. To narrow your focus, you need a premise.

It is important to note, in academic writing, a good premise is not a hard fact, but rather something provable. It is something readers will be persuaded to accept by the time they finish reading. *The Axis Powers lost World War II* is not a premise. It is a fact. *The Axis Powers lost World War II because they were not a true alliance* is a premise. It is a statement that can be proven (or disproven).

To determine a premise using a mind map, follow these steps:

1. Write in the center the general subject about which you want to or are assigned to write.

2. Jot down all your knowledge about the subject around the center. This is going to be a brain dump of everything you know or can recall about the subject.

3. Look at the items you dumped on the map and see if any relationships or correlations jump out that you would enjoy discussing or elaborating. Note them as subset or second level branches.

4. Examine each statement and pick the one that will be the most enjoyable or practical for the assignment.

To illustrate, we'll go back to our example. You have been assigned to write a paper about World War II. At the present moment, you don't a have premise, so you sit down with a blank paper and a pen. In the center of the paper you write *World War II* as that is the subject you have been asked to cover.

Then you write anything that you know and remember about the war. You might jot down countries and alliances involved in the war. You may note its important dates and events. You can also include the major leaders and historical figures. You connect these ideas to the central topic.

Next look carefully at what you have written. Try to see if any interesting relationships exist. You may look at the list of countries and think certain ones were critical to certain events transpiring or not transpiring. You may look at events and reflect how their occurrence or non-occurrence may have impacted the war. You may even analyze the personality of the leaders and determine how their character or temperament may have influenced their decision making. Note the relationships next to the appropriate branch.

Finally go through and examine each relationship to determine which one will be the most practical for the assignment at hand. Once you pick a statement, you will have a clear and provable premise. You will have an argument towards which to direct your writing, making it easier to read and understand.

This step is great for academic writing like essays, dissertations, or critiques. It is also great for article writers who have to generate unique content for magazines or blogs. Now that you have a premise or foundation for your writing, it's time to develop your points.

Step 2. Developing the Key Points

As mentioned, the key points support your premise. When you have well developed and thought-out key points, your writing will flow, from one point to the next, making your reader more readily accept your premise. This organization is critical to creating effective writing. After all, it doesn't matter how hard you punch, if you never hit the target.

To develop the key points, follow these steps:

1. Start with the premise of the project in the center.

2. Determine the facts, issues, and arguments you want to discuss about the premise. Create a subtopic for each item of discussion.

3. Using subset branches, plan out all the specifics about each fact, issue, or argument. If it is a large project, like a book or business plan, you may wish to create a separate Mind Map for each key subtopic and let these be the chapters or sections of your work.

4. Once you have a complete mind map with your points, pick a subtopic to start writing—you don't need

to write them in order. Sometimes it is easiest to start at the end of a writing project and work backwards.

5. As you write, check off subsets on your Mind Map that you have addressed.

6. When all the subsets of a subtopic are checked off, you have finished that subtopic.

7. Write a conclusion for that section of your project and move on to the next subtopic.

Let's go back to the World War II example. You used the first mind map to come up with several possible premises for an essay about the war. You picked one, *British home front support was critical to the Allied victory*. Now you create another mind map to develop your points

First you write the central idea, *Home Front Support Critical to Victory*. Around the central idea, you write the things British citizens did that impacted the war effort. These will be your key points. Around each key point, write one of two things: evidence for how this point impacted the war effort or what made this point important to the war. When you are done, you have a collection of facts to support each point.

When you go through all the points, you will have an organized essay with each idea pointing towards the premise to support how the British home front was critical to the Allied victory.

Step 3. Reviewing the Draft

Of course, even the best writers don't get everything perfect the first time. This is why authors write multiple drafts and publishers hire editors. For the rest of us, there is review.

Just as Mind Mapping can be used before and during the actual writing, it can be used after when reviewing. As we stated, integrating a Mind Map into the review step allows you to perfect your focus and organization. Let's take a look at how you can use the technique to make review effective.

1. Again, write the premise in the center of the paper.

2. Read through each paragraph or section, write its key point as a subtopic, and draw a line connecting it to the premise.

3. Read the sentences of each paragraph or section. Each sentence should be able to connect to the key point. If a sentence does not connect to the key point, either *modify*, *move*, or *remove* the sentence to a different part of the essay.

Modify - You probably have a handful of sentences not written or stated properly. Modify these sentences so they more clearly reinforce the key point. Write the modified version on the review Mind Map as a sub-branch under the subtopic.

Move - You likely also have a handful of sentences that actually connect to ideas in different paragraphs. Move these sentences to where you feel they will be better served. Place the sentence as a subset branch in the subtopic where you want the sentence moved.

Remove - You may still have some ideas that don't connect to anything. Don't place these sentences in the review Mind Map. Simply cross them off the article.

4. After completing this for all the paragraphs or sections, you will have a visual diagram of the changes that need to be made. Go through each branch and take the newly organized sentences and drop them in the article in the appropriate paragraph or section.

When you are done, you will have a final draft with each sentence in your article connecting to the key points and the key points reinforcing the overall premise. Anything that doesn't support the premise or anything that dilutes the focus has been either modified or removed. What is left is purposeful and directed writing.

This is the general approach to writing with Mind Maps. It is a great aid to writers and should actually precede the writing process, even if you have the desire to get started quickly. Using it will prove helpful, particularly if you find outlines too constricting or suppressive to idea expansion.

Brainstorming

There is a popular kids' show that introduces the idea of brainstorming. When the characters brainstorm, a rain cloud (complete with rain) blows in and random objects (ideas) pop out of the cloud. Usually, these ideas have no relation to what they are brainstorming. Then the storm ends, and all of a sudden the characters have a fully-fledged idea.

Sometimes, it feels like that is exactly what brainstorming is supposed to be. You conjure up a frenzy of thoughts and all kinds of things pop into your head and then—out of nowhere—you have an idea!

Of course, as many people have learned, brainstorming doesn't work that way. Random thoughts don't lead anywhere unless they are connected and pulled together in some way. Mind Maps are great for brainstorming because they help you pull together and find connections between thoughts to help you come up with and generate new ideas.

Here's how it works:

1. Put the topic of the brainstorm in the center of the sheet. When writing the topic, try to be as specific as possible. For example, if you are brainstorming gift ideas for your daughter Lisa, instead of saying *Brainstorm* or *Gift Ideas*, write *Christmas Gift Ideas for Lisa*. The more specific you can make your topic, the more your mind can focus on a precise solution.

2. Gaze at the central topic and write down any ideas that come to mind. Set these as subtopics and connect them to the center with a branch. Unlike in other areas like writing or note taking, don't over think or over analyze the subtopics. The goal of brainstorming is to get your thoughts circulating. The more your thoughts are circulating, the more ideas and potential solutions you can generate. The best way to get your thoughts circulating is to jot down what comes to mind as they come up without censoring them.

3. Glance over each subtopic and see what ideas they bring to mind. Write new ideas down as a subset and connect them to the subtopics that triggered the ideas. Again do not censor your thoughts. Just allow them to flow and have everything come out. The censoring will come later.

4. Repeat step 3 for the subsets, creating branches into lower and lower levels. Once you have gone as deep as

you can go, you will have a detailed Mind Map with several levels of ideas. Some of the ideas will be related to the topic while much of them will be completely unrelated.

5. Scan through the map and see which ideas might be useful or worth pursuing. Note the useful ones by putting an asterisk next to them. You may even decide to add sub-branches to record important details about how to cultivate or advance the idea. Here you can censor your thoughts to really analyze and work things through.

6. After detailing an idea with sub-branches, you may find that it doesn't serve your needs. You can cross it off and move to the next.

Below is a demonstration of how a brainstorm mind map might come together. This map used the example in the beginning of the section to generate ideas for a Christmas gift.

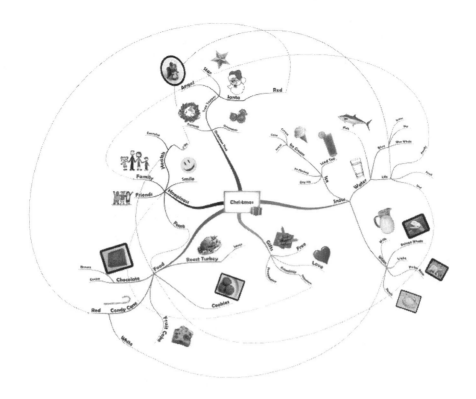

Looking up, you'll notice we put *Christmas* with a giftwrapped box next to it. From here, we let our thoughts flow. Christmas initially got us thinking about *Snow*, *Gifts*, *Food*, *Christmas Tree*, and *Happiness*, so we wrote these as subtopics. We did not censor our thoughts; we simply wrote what came to mind.

Considering these entries got our brain thinking about related entries. *Christmas Tree* got us thinking about tree toppers like *garlands*, *ornaments*, *angels*, and *stars*. *Food* got us thinking about *candy canes*, *chocolates*, and *cookies*. *Snow* got us thinking about *ice*, *water*, and the *color white*. We went further down with *white* and *wrote pearls, polar bear,* and *beluga whale,* as these are all items that are white.

With our thoughts and ideas flushed out, we can look at the map and see if any gift ideas pop up. Right away we spot some potential ideas like *chocolate* and *pearls*; and although an actual polar bear is not feasible, a stuffed one might be.

Here we create sub-branches within each one of these ideas to further analyze. We may think that chocolate is a good option because we know Lisa loves chocolate; therefore we can put an asterisk next to chocolate, and with sub-branches, note the type of chocolates or the specific brands she likes. We might conclude that pearls are unreasonable for a child and probably out of our budget. This we can cross off the map as a potential solution. As mentioned, although a polar bear is not feasible, a stuffed animal would be a great idea. We can list ideas for possible stuffed animals. We continue this process with other ideas.

Some ideas we come across can trigger a whole host of other possibilities. For example, examining *beluga whale* might trigger us to think about marine life, which may trigger us to think about the marine life at the local aquarium. If Lisa loves the aquarium, a weekend excursion might also be a worthwhile gift. As new ideas come up, we can extended branches to develop them as if they were part of the original Mind Map.

It is important to note, as you analyze the map, solutions will come up a few ways. You may come up with multiple solutions, from which you pick the one you like best. In this example, we came up with *chocolate*, *stuffed animal*, and *aquarium*. From these choices, we pick the most suitable gift given our requirements and constraints. Alternatively, you may come up with a bunch of related ideas that combine to form one great idea. In one branch, we listed *family* and *friends*, in another, *aquarium*, yet another, *Santa*. We might combine them and decide to have an outing at the aquarium inviting Lisa's family and friends, while hiring or dressing up as Santa to hand out presents. This is another admirable solution.

If you don't get worthwhile solutions or ideas in the first go, you can repeat the steps to generate an additional set of thoughts. You can start with a new Mind Map or expand the current one. Either way, repeat this process as often as you need until you are satisfied with the results of your brainstorm.

This is a handy way to brainstorm with Mind Maps. As you have learned, our thoughts are not linear. As a result, ideas and solutions do not come out of our heads linearly, one after another. They come out as illustrated in the brainstorm Mind Map, in layers and levels, with some ideas related to the topic while many completely unrelated. Often the perfect idea will not be staring you in the face. It will need to be massaged until it is just right. The design of a Mind Map allows you to capture potential ideas and work through them to give you the perfect solution or solutions you need.

Decision Making

Decision making is the process of evaluating available options and selecting a course of action. Over your personal and professional life, you will be faced with an abundance of decisions—picking the right job, choosing the best school, opting for the safest procedure.

Decision making is a critical life skill. If you can make intelligent, well-informed decisions, then you can avoid costly and time consuming mistakes. As a leader, good decision-making skills will help you guide you or your team to well-deserved success.

As critical as this skill is, though, it can be difficult and scary. Decisions come with many outcomes and scenarios to consider. They also close the door on at least one possibility, and in many ways, commit you to a specific path, a path of which you may not know the outcome. It's no wonder that many feel like deer in headlights when confronted with a decision.

Fortunately, there are Mind Maps. Mind Maps are fantastic in this area because they allow you to create a visual image of the decision you are facing. By laying out your decision in visual form, you can better analyze all the available options and the positive and negatives of each one. This makes it easier to see the best course of action. Since the best choice is easy to recognize, much of the anxiety associated with making a decision is removed. You are not driving yourself crazy by replaying endless what if scenarios in your head. Often, the best choice is obvious and apparent.

You'll find that mind mapping a decision is surprisingly simple. To begin, write the decision you are considering in the middle of a piece of paper. Making a decision usually requires examining a set of options, so in a circular fashion around the decision, write the different options you are evaluating. Draw a line connecting each option to the center, so you can see they are directly related to the decision.

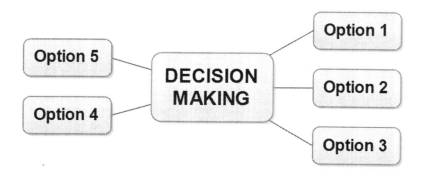

Next, create two subset branches for each option. Label one *Pro* and label the other *Con*. Your mind map should look as follows. This will be the starting point for your decision making.

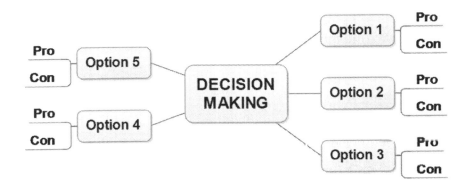

Now, under each *Pro* branch, write all the positives or benefits of the option. It helps to think in terms of what you will gain from choosing that option. Likewise, under each *Con* branch, write the negative aspects or costs associated with making that decision. It helps to think of *Cons* in terms of what you will or have to give up. Come up with as many pros and cons about each option, and note them in the appropriate branch.

When doing this, make sure to include only the pros and cons that are important or relevant to you or for the decision at hand. Including ancillary points will not be helpful here. In the course of this process, if you included items that are insignificant or trivial, you can remove or cross them off the map. Once you add the pros and cons, you will have a map that looks like so:

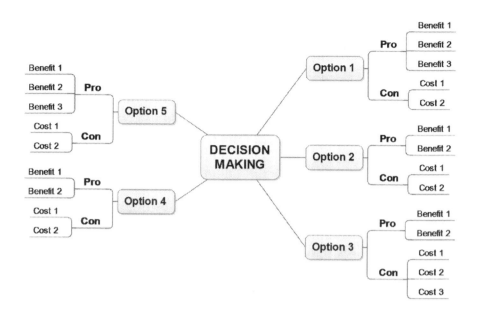

Here you have the decisions all laid out. You can clearly see every option and the advantages and disadvantages of each one. All the relevant information is right in front of you. More importantly, the diagram is free from immaterial or extraneous details that can clutter your head and unnecessarily complicate the decision. From here, it's simply a matter of evaluating the pros and cons and choosing the one that is right for you.

To help in the evaluation, you can quantify your decision. That is, you can score each option by applying a numbering system to the *Pros* and *Cons*. For example, you can give a rating from +1 to +5 to each item you listed as a *Pro*. If the pro is a major advantage, rate it +5. If it is a minor advantage, rate it +1. For anything in between, use a scale from +2 to +4.

Do the same for the *Con* items, but rate them from -1 to -5. If a *Con* is a major issue, give it -5. For minor issues, assign a rating of -1. For anything in between, use -2 to -4.

Then add up all the numbers you assigned to each option. For example, under *Option 1*, you may have listed three *Pros* with the following ratings: +2, +1, and +4 for a total of +7. You may have also listed two *Cons* with ratings of -3 and -2 for a total of -5. The net comes to 7 + -5 = 2. That is the score for *Option 1*. You do this for all the other options, and the one with the highest score will likely be your best choice.

Now, not all of your decision making will require you to narrow your choices down to one selection. Sometimes you will need to select two or three options from a list. In this case, the two or three with the highest scores are going to be the best picks. At other times, you will be required to eliminate the least appealing option. This will be the one that scores the lowest. At still other times, you will need to pick between the lesser of several negative possibilities, so you would pick the one with the lowest negative score.

Furthermore, as you are scoring the pros and cons, you may come across an item that is a deal breaker. For example, you may be a graduating high school student deciding between four universities to attend the following year. While listing the benefits of each university, you realize that option 3 does not offer a scholarship. The last thing you want is to come out of school with a lot of debt, so lack of financial assistance is not negotiable. When you come across a deal breaker, cross that option off your map entirely. This lightens the mental load in the decision-making process.

Of course, not all decisions will be this straightforward. Some decisions will have fears and apprehensions behind them, especially personal issues that involve relationships and life changes. These things can't easily be put into a pro or con nor quantified into a numerical scale. For example, you may be deciding between three job offers. After listing the tangible positive and negatives such as salary, commute time, and title, you come across some worries. In considering one job, you are unsure of your ability to perform. Another job raises the question of the stability of the position or company altogether. You fear that either of these two options may have the potential to leave you unemployed 3-6 months down the road.

At initial glance, these concerns may seem like negatives or *cons*; however, they are only possibilities. Your performance may very well be fine or the company may very well have a long and bright future. Thus there is a likelihood that the events you fear may not transpire. Nonetheless, you still need a way to incorporate these concerns into your evaluation.

You can incorporate issues and fears like these into a decision-making Mind Map by adding them as a separate subset of the option. Then with sub-branches, you can work out the details of the issue or fear. In the sub-branches, you can list things causing the fear or ways to help overcome it. A mentor once taught me that to overcome indecision caused by fear, think about what you would do if the thing you fear transpired. That is, what actions would you take to rectify the situation if the outcome you fear occurs? Adding this to the map will give it this appearance:

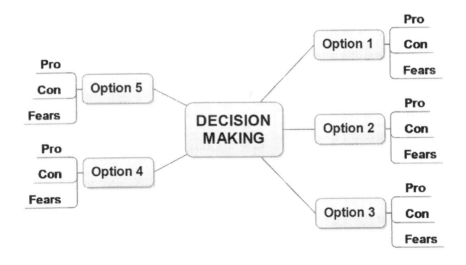

As you can see, this diagram takes the previous map and adds a sub-branch labeled *fears* to each option. This addition enhances our decision making by allowing us to better assess potential problems that may arise down the road from a particular option.

To enhance our decision-making Mind Map further, we can add sub-branches to each option. We live in a world of options. Some of our options in themselves have options. For example, if I were in the market to purchase a tablet P.C., I could buy one from Amazon, Apple, Google, or Samsung. My options don't end here. Amazon models include 7" and 8.9". Apple has similar varieties in the iPad and iPad mini. Google and Samsung have even more. We can list these as second-level branches within the main options. Here is an illustration:

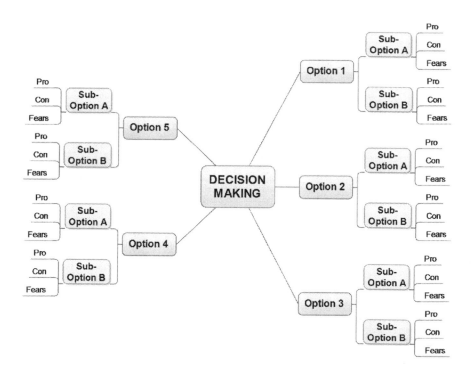

Here we have a Mind Map with first-level branches that list our options. Within the second-level branches are the sub-options. The third level has branches for pros and cons, as well as any fears and concerns. With all this, we have an in-depth decision-making Mind Map that gives us the ability to look at and analyze many pieces of information.

With this diagram, you can really see the flexibility of mind mapping for decision making. You can keep it simple with only pros and cons or complex by adding sub-options and fears and concerns. If you wanted, you could add even more layers. We mentioned that Amazon has 7" and 8.9" Kindle models. Within those models you have choices for Wifi Only or 3G, 16GB or 32GB. We could create additional layers for the additional options and choices we might encounter. Mind Maps allow you to go as in-depth into a decision as you need.

This method works really well if you already know all the options available to you. Sometimes, however, you will not have this information off hand. In fact, you may not have any information. In these cases, you will need to do some research before starting the map. As you uncover options, you can list them in the mind map.

To illustrate with a real world decision, let's take Howard. Howard is in the market for a new car. He wants a good reliable vehicle, for a good price, that is fuel efficient and can comfortably seat his wife and three children. He decides to look into purchasing a mid-sized, four-door sedan. He doesn't know much about cars, so he goes on line to see his available options.

He knows there will be a lot to take in, so he starts a Mind Map. In the middle, he puts *new car purchase*. As he comes across potential options, he creates branches and puts them on the map as subtopics.

The first car he comes across is the Toyota Corolla. This fits the description for what he is looking. He notices the Corolla comes in three versions—*L*, *LE*, and *S*. The *L* is a base model with fewer features, and the *S* is a higher-end model with upgrades. He adds *Corolla* as a subtopic and the three versions as subsets.

He searches for Corolla's competitors and comes across the Honda Civic and Ford Focus. The Civic comes in *LX*, *EX*, and *EX-L* versions and the Focus in *S*, *SE*, and *ST*. He adds both to his map.

He searches some more and discovers the Hyndai Elantra. This model comes in *L*, *GL*, and *GLS*. He notes this on the diagram. There is one more model in which he is interested, the Nissan Sentra, which comes in *S*, *FE*, and *SV*. He notes this too. Right now, Howard's map looks like this:

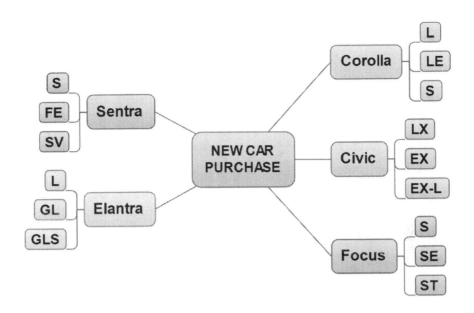

This map has 5 subtopics, one for each model Howard is evaluating – *Corolla*, *Civic*, *Focus*, *Elantra*, and *Sentra*. Within each model, he has listed the versions that are available. We can add more models to the list, but this is a good starting point for Howard. These cars are all in the same class, price range, and with similar build, engine size, and fuel economy.

Within each version, he creates 3 additional branches— one titled *price*, one titled *specifications*, and another titled *features*. Under *price*, he lists the MSRP of the car as well as any cash backs or incentives the manufacturer offers. Under *specifications*, he lists the engine size, number of cylinders, and miles per gallon. Under *features* he lists options that come with that particular brand like power windows, power locks, sun roof, etc. He may even opt to create a sub-branch titled *upgrades*, to list enhancements that don't come standard with each version and its cost.

Now Howard has a valuable starting point. Instead of shuffling through all the varieties in his head, he has it all arranged in a diagram. He doesn't have to think *Wait, is the LX a version of the Corolla or the Civic? Is it the Sentra that comes with standard moon roof or the Elantra?* All the information is in front of him, including prices, specifications, features, and upgrades. From here he can analyze the options and determine the best choice given his budget and needs.

Notice this Mind Map doesn't list pros and cons or fears. That is because it doesn't really need to. The features and specifications essentially highlight the pros and cons of each model. In this particular example, Howard could avoid the *Pro & Con* step, though, if he wanted, he could still give a number rating to all the specs and features to quantify the value of each model. The model with the most points would likely be his best choice.

This is the approach to making a decision with Mind Maps. To list step by step:

1. Start with your available options. If you don't know what is available, do some research.

2. If your options have sub-options, as with the car example, list them under each option.

3. From here you can do one of two things: List pros and cons or list specs and features of each option.

4. If you have anxiety about the decision, you can add a branch for fears and apprehensions you have about each option. You can work out the fear with sub-branches.

5. Analyze what you have listed and come to a decision. To help with the analysis, you can quantify it by employing a numbering system. The option or options with the highest number will likely be your best choice.

Planning

Planning is the act of organizing and thinking through all the activities required to achieve a desired goal. When creating a plan, it helps to be able to put it all down on paper before you start. Many people use outlines or lists to plan, but you can use Mind Maps as well. For many plans, Mind Maps work better than the alternatives.

They work better because they allow you to jump from one step to another freely. A linear way of planning has you focus on one item at a time. It forces you that you plan out step 1 before moving to step 2 and so on. However, the mind doesn't work that way; it jumps all over the place, going from one idea to another. When you are planning, it is helps to be able to jump around.

This way when you have a great idea, you can note it down in the proper place before you lose it.

Consider a family planning a vacation. They are going on a weeklong road trip and stopping in a different place each day. If they plan their trip as an outline, they start with day 1 to decide what they are going to do that day. Then they go on to day 2, and so on.

What if, in the middle of planning day 1, someone has a great idea for what to do on day 4, when they will be visiting Aunt Susie? There is nowhere to put it on the outline because they haven't gotten to day 4 yet. They can make a side note or hope that someone remembers the idea. However, too many side notes will jumble your thoughts and clutter your outline.

If instead they used a Mind Map, they could start with a main idea *Road Trip*. Then they would branch out subtopics of *Day 1, Day 2, Day 3*, and so on. Around each subtopic they would fill in how far they will drive that day, fun things to do, places where they will eat, and more. If someone remembers a good restaurant in the area of Day 5, they wouldn't have to make a side note or try to hold on to the idea; instead, they could immediately add it to that branch.

Here is a suggested step-by-step process for planning with a Mind Map:

1. Create your Mind Map with the main idea being the project you are planning.

2. Figure out all the steps that need to be taken or all the items that need to be handled. For a road trip, the major steps can be what you will do each day, *Day 1, Day 2, Day 3*; or the main destinations you will visit, *Grand Canyon, Yosemite Park, Lake Tahoe*. For events like a party, items to work through may include the venue, guest list, decoration, etc. If you are putting together a business plan, your strategy might involve employees, marketing, budget, accounting, etc.

3. Set these major steps as your subtopics.

4. Starting with the first major step, try to think of as many smaller steps as you can.

5. Write down the smaller steps as subsets of the first major step.

6. If you get an idea for smaller steps on other subtopics, write them down as they occur and then go back to the step you were working on.

7. When you have broken down the process as far as you can and have written down every step you can think of, read it over and sleep on it.

8. Come back later and read it again, making sure you didn't miss anything and that everything is where it belongs.

When you are done, you'll have a complete Mind Map showing everything you need to complete your project.

We will use planning a road trip as an example to illustrate quickly. You have a week off work and you'd like to spend that time by taking a road trip with your family. You and your family gather around the coffee table to schedule the vacation. Since you want to reserve the last day as a relaxation day to recuperate from the trip and get back into your regular routine, you have six days to plan out. You choose to plan the trip by day, so you begin as follows.

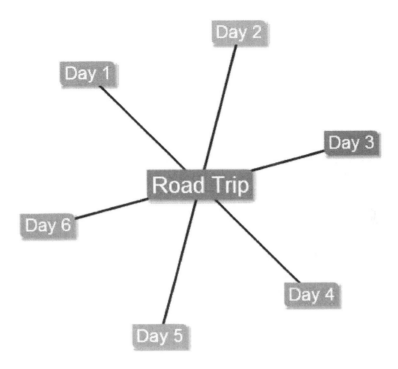

Looking above, we have Road Trip in the center, with Day 1 through Day 6 as subtopics around the center. From here, you can plan out the details of what to do each day.

For a plan like this, more than likely, each day will require you to choose or make a similar set of decisions. Whether you are on day 2 or day 5, you will need to decide what *activities* you are going to do, the *distance* you are going to drive, where you will *lodge* to spend the night, what *foods* you are going to eat, and most importantly, the major sites and *attractions* you plan on seeing. Since you will need to make these decisions for all of the days, it will help to establish them as subsets in your map as follows.

Examining the above picture, you will notice we added the subsets of Activities, Distance, Lodging, Food, and Attractions around each of the days. These are the typical items we want to consider for our family road trip. If you wanted to include other items such as budget, you could add them as well.

Now that you have a framework laid out of what you are going to be doing and when, you can start planning the individual aspects of the trip. You can go through each day and choose the attractions you will see, the activities you will do, the distance you will drive, and the places you will eat for that day. If an idea for a different day pops up, you can note it accordingly without worrying about losing that thought.

This is planning with Mind Maps. Planning is a broad field that covers a wide variety of activities. As a result, the purpose of this section was to give you a general overview. This way, you can get a sense of how to use the system in this area and begin applying it with different types of plans. In the next section, we discuss a more specialized and complicated form of planning called project management.

Project Management

Project management is the process of bringing together people and resources to achieve an objective. Managing a project can be a surprisingly difficult endeavor. That's because projects have many unique and individual parts and components, like gears in a clock, that need to work together cohesively and function as a whole. Due to the numerous pieces involved, it can be challenging to know if the correct pieces are in place and whether they are working toward the end goal.

This intrinsic challenge of project management is what Mind Maps handle best. They take large and complex tasks and break them down so they are easier to manage. Their web-like structure of outer and inner branches break activities by both hierarchy and function. This way it is easy to see how each part of a project comes together to make the whole and how the whole serves each of the individual parts. If there is a piece that is out of place, it is easy to detect and isolate. If a piece is missing, it can be identified at the onset, instead of later on when making major changes become difficult.

To create a project management Mind Map, follow these steps:

1. Write the name of the project as the main topic. If the project does not have a name yet or one at all, use something that defines the project or what it is trying to achieve. This is important as it keeps the core objective in view at all times.

2. Break the project down into major or high level activities. Add branches for each activity and connect them to the main topic. These will be the subtopics. Don't add low-level tasks and responsibilities here. The aim is to create a pecking order.

3. Break the high-level activities into lower-level tasks and responsibilities. To do this, think about all the errands, chores, roles, and duties required to achieve each activity. It helps to think of each high-level activity or subtopic as a mini Mind Map. Connect these lower level tasks with subset branches to the subtopic.

4. Depending on the size of the project, divide the lower-level tasks further. Truncate into lower and lower levels to ensure all aspects of the project is noted. At this stage, you will have a big picture view of the project with all the detailed level tasks that need to get done.

5. Establish due dates for all the tasks and activities. For each branch, whether it is a subtopic, subset, or one lower in the chain, label when it should be completed. This can be done either top-down or bottom-up. Top-down means looking at when the overall project needs to be completed and working down setting dates of the individual activities and tasks to ensure the principal end date can be met. Bottom-up means starting with due dates of individual tasks and activities and working up to determine the earliest point the project can be completed.

6. If necessary, add comments, remarks, or important reminders next to the tasks and activities. For example, if some tasks have special approval or handling requirements, you can note them appropriately. If some tasks require that others be finished first, and therefore will have their start date delayed if other ones aren't completed, you can note that as well. This will keep you aware of important considerations.

7. Finally, assign people, groups, and departments responsible for each task or activity. Next to each

branch you can put names or pictures of people who are the lead for each branch or assigned to each task. They will be the point of contact to ensure things are moving along smoothly.

These are the basic steps of creating a project management Mind Map. To demonstrate, let's look at Actel LTD, a national manufacturing company headquartered in Chicago, Illinois. Due to increased competition, the company is forced to lower overhead costs. The lease on the corporate office is running out, so one way they've decided to reduce overhead is to relocate across state into a cheaper office space.

Due to the size of the company, this will be a big project to tackle. Senior management wants to ensure everything is in order before beginning so they create a project management Mind Map. In the center they write *Relocate Corporate Office* as that sums up the goal of the project.

After careful consideration, they determine the move will involve managing 5 separate and distinct activities– *Open New Office*, *Close Old Office*, *Relocate Employees*, *Move Equipment and Supplies*, and *Notify of Address Change*. They write this as first-level branches around the main topic as follows:

Then they think through and jot down all the individual tasks that need to be accomplished for each activity. For opening a new office, senior management decides they need to perform the following tasks: *find available space to rent, negotiate price, add leasehold improvements, establish floor plan*, and *set up utilities*. For closing the old office, they agree they need to *cancel utilities, remove leasehold improvements, clean office space*, and *hand over keys*. They do this for the rest of the activities to produce the following Mind Map.

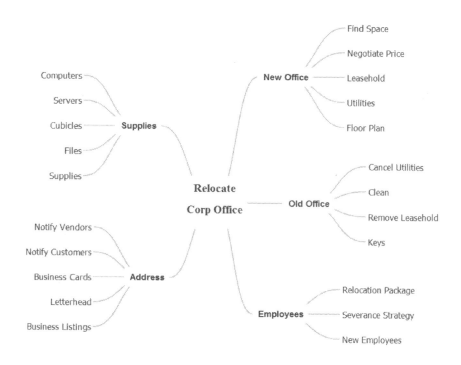

From here they truncate into lower and lower levels. They break down each task into more specific errands, jobs, and duties. For example, the task of moving the cubicles requires the cubicles to be *uninstalled*, *packed*, *shipped to the new address*, and *reinstalled*. They note this around the sub-branch off *Cubicles*. To move files, they need to *purchase boxes*, *put files into boxes*, *label the boxes*, and *ship to the new office*. They note these items within the branch for *Files*. They continue this for all the activities and tasks until they are satisfied with the level of detail.

Now comes the timeline and due dates. The summer months are the least busy for the company, so management decides to begin the move in June with its completion no later than August 31. Based on this, they decide the 5 main activities need to be completed by August 15th. With this end date in mind, they assign due dates to all of the individual tasks and errands to ensure the August 15th deadline can be met.

As they assign due dates, they also jot comments and remarks around selected tasks and activities. They note that customers and vendors can't be notified of the new address until an office space is found. They also note the old office space can't be cleaned until the leasehold improvements are removed. More importantly, they note no lease agreement can be accepted without the approval of the President.

Finally they assign people and groups to each activity. They assign the activity of relocating employees to the HR department, with Jenny, the HR director, as the lead. The task of negotiating pricing is assigned to Carl in Legal. Cleaning the old office space is the responsibility of maintenance, and the responsibility of shipping files belongs to the Admin department.

Completing the above steps gives senior management a very effective execution strategy. They can look at the map and see exactly what needs to be done, by whom, and when. They can insert into the map any fragments that are missing and any tasks that need to be broken down further can be done here and now. As the project gets under way, they can reference the diagram to ensure all tasks and activities are moving along smoothly. If setbacks arise, they can approach the assigned person or group about the issue.

Categorizing the main branches by major activities is one approach to managing a project with Mind Maps. There are other ways to arrange the main branches. Instead of major activities, you may opt to divide the branches into phases—*Phase I, Phase II, Phase III*—as in the illustration below. This is great for managing construction type projects.

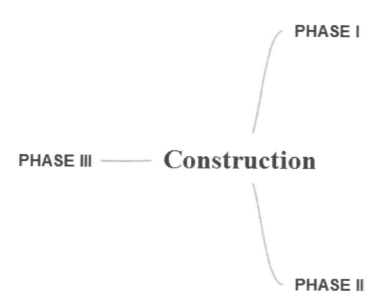

Another way to subdivide the main branch is by Department. This works well in corporate settings. Here is an illustration.

Yet another option is to begin with people working on the project. This is great for school projects or when you are working in a small group that does not deal with high-level activities, phases, or departments.

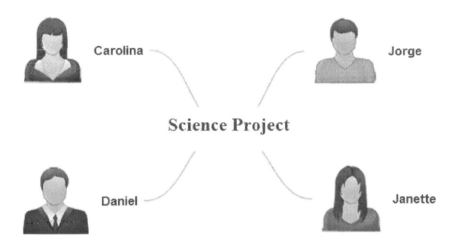

Before breaking a project down, you may need to do some preliminary evaluation like analyzing resources, constraints, risk, etc. You can begin a Mind Map as illustrated below. This is the standard textbook method of managing a project taught in business school.

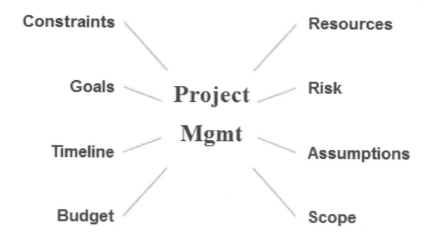

These are some different ways to start the main branches. No matter what starting point you use, how you proceed will remain the same. You break large tasks and activities into smaller parts until everything you want to manage is noted.

Estimating Project Time

This is one of the simplest and most useful things you can do with a Mind Map. As long as you know how to construct a Mind Map, you can estimate project time for anything.

To start, follow the directions on using Mind Maps for planning or project management. Then follow these steps:

1. Make an estimate of how long each subset will take to complete.

2. Add up all your subsets and you have an estimate for each subtopic.

3. The total for your subtopics is the estimated time for the entire project.

4. Add a cushion to allow for delays, unexpected problems, and acts of God.

Why does this work so well? The brain is really good at grasping and estimating small concrete things—for instance, how long it will take to write a five-page report. It gets harder to estimate the larger the task gets, and the less concrete—for instance, how long will it take to plan and implement an organizational overhaul of the marketing department.

Making time estimates on the subsets of a Mind Maps is something your brain can do easily. Then you just add those estimates together (always adding some extra time as a safety net) and you have a good approximation for your entire project.

Problem Solving

There is something about being faced with a difficult problem that can just make the mind freeze up. Whether it is a result of stress, not knowing where to start, or not being entirely sure of the underlining cause, problem solving can be far more difficult than it needs to be.

Mind Maps can make problem solving easier for several reasons. First, they make the problem visual, which helps you better understand it. Second, they organize your thoughts, so you can focus your thinking on specific issues. Lastly, they let you see everything that is involved, ensuring your solutions in one area don't create problems in another.

Problem solving works best if you can relax. When you worry, you don't think about the problem you are trying to solve; instead, you think about the bad things that will happen if you don't come up with a solution. When you get ready to make your Mind Map, make sure you are calm and thinking about solutions, not focusing on your worries.

Problem solving with Mind Maps, step-by-step:

1. Make the problem the main topic of the Mind Map.

2. Take a few minutes to think about the different parts of the problem.

3. Make the different parts of the problem the subtopics.

4. Include details about each part of the problem as subsets.

5. Once you have detailed the problem as much as possible, start looking for solutions or possibilities for addressing each subset. Try using a brainstorm Mind Map to come up with ideas.

6. Next to each subset or subtopic, write down a possible solution to that part of the problem.

7. Don't worry if possible solutions don't all work together; just get as many options as you can down.

8. Once you've gotten solutions for as much of the problem as you can, spend some time thinking about your options.

9. Pick a solution or group of solutions to your problem that you think will work best.

10. Use the guidelines for planning with Mind Maps to plan out your solution.

Here is an example to demonstrate. Joan and Dave are having money trouble. They don't have enough in their budget to cover all their expenses. Dave is working full time and Joan part time.

The main topic of their Mind Map will be *money troubles*. After talking, they realize there are three parts to their difficulty—not enough income, too many expenses, and no savings. These become their subtopics.

Off of *income* they make subsets for each of their incomes. Off of *expenses* they make subsets for everything they spend money on—utilities, cost of living (food, clothes, gas, etc.), and entertainment. Off of *no savings*, they make a subset for *unexpected expenses* and *retirement*, the two main reasons they need savings. Their initial Mind Map looks like this.

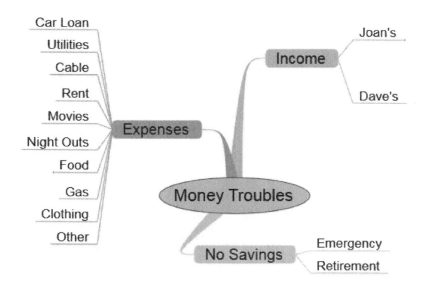

Now they start looking for solutions. Joan could ask her boss about getting more hours or going full time. Dave could ask for a raise. They could start a home business. Either or both of them could look for a better-paying job. As far as expenses, they can refinance loans with lower payments, cut unnecessary expenditures, and choose lower-cost options. For retirement, they can start making a habit of setting aside 3% of each pay check for savings, no matter what bills don't get paid. Even better, they can open a 401k, so the funds are set aside tax free. Joan could go back to school and get a vocational degree. Joan and Dave add all of these ideas to their Mind Map as follows.

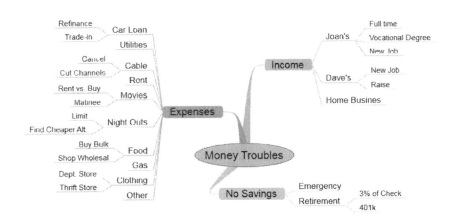

Once they come up with as many solutions as they can think of, they pick a few that they like. Joan will look into home businesses she can run in addition to her part-time job. Dave will look for a job with better pay. They will make some lifestyle changes to cut expenses, and half of what Joan brings in with her home business will go directly into a new savings account.

You can use the same process on almost any problem. Just take your time, don't let worries overwhelm you, and use the Mind Map to break the problem down into small sections.

Diagnosis

Diagnosis is the process of identifying the source of a problem or condition out of a list of probable alternatives. When people think of diagnosis, they usually think of doctors and psychologists diagnosing physical and mental ailments. Although the medical profession is one area where diagnosis is performed, other professions employ it as well. It is performed by mechanics when they look under the hood of a car or by computer technicians when they examine a computer problem. Most customer service representatives perform diagnosis when trying to resolve customer complaints.

Like other areas we've discussed, Mind Maps are an effective diagnostic tool. The technique makes it easy to gather symptoms, determine possible causes, and narrow in on a precise source or cause of a problem, all in one place.

To perform diagnosis with mind maps, apply these steps:

1. Gather information about the problem or complaint such as symptoms, history, etc.

2. Based on the information gathered, make a list of probable causes. Put these items around the center as first-level branches on the map.

3. For each probable cause, determine additional signs and symptoms that need to be observed to confirm the particular cause. Set these as second-level branches.

4. List questions that need to be asked or tests and actions that need to be performed to confirm existence of the symptoms. Record these as third-level branches around the symptom.

5. Beginning with the most common or likely cause, ask the necessary questions or perform the necessary tests and actions to determine existence or non-existence of the symptoms. Note the result or outcome in the appropriate place on the map.

6. Based on the results of the tests, rule out each cause until you narrow in on the most likely one.

Here we go with an example. For this section, we are going to play doctor. A patient walks into the office complaining of knee pain. To diagnose the pain, we first gather preliminary information about the patient, like his age, weight, and medical history, and the pain, like when it first came about and whether the patient had recently done extraneous activity.

Based on the health and age of the patient, we eliminate some ailments off the bat, like arthritis or bone fracture, as possible causes of the pain. The patient acknowledges to performing more than the usual amount of physical activity over the past few days, so we determine it to likely be an overuse injury to the cartilage, muscle, tendon, or ligament. Given this, we concluded the pain to be caused either by a *meniscus tear*, *tendinitis*, or *Iliotibial Band Syndrome*. We commence our map like so:

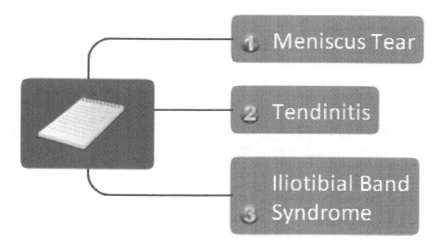

In this Mind Map, we began with the possible causes of the patient's pain around the center. We narrowed down to three possibilities, so we placed three subtopics stemming from the center.

If you notice, we left the main topic blank. The main topic is not required when performing a diagnosis as we don't have an exact issue to work on. Putting something might lead us in the wrong direction. For example, if we put *Knee Pain Diagnosis*, we might unconsciously focus solely on knee-related issues and miss other probable causes that are not directly related to the knee, but can still cause pain in the region. Instead of putting something that might lead us in the wrong direction, its best to leave it blank. If you feel the need to put something, you can put the name of the person, object, or system you are diagnosing. In this case we can put the patient's name.

For each ailment, we list the additional symptoms we ought to observe. A meniscal tear exhibits sensation of the knee "giving way," inflammation of the joint lining, inability to straighten the knee, as well as a click, pop, or locking of the knee. Symptoms of tendinitis are associated with pain in the quadriceps muscle, pain performing activities such as running, jumping, or squatting, difficulty bending the knee, and damage to the patellar tendon. Signs of Iliotibial Band Syndrome consist of pain on the side of the knee, pain up the side of the thigh, a thickened iliotibial band, and are usually common in people who have a discrepancy in the length of their leg. We write these symptoms as second-level branches next to the respective ailment like so:

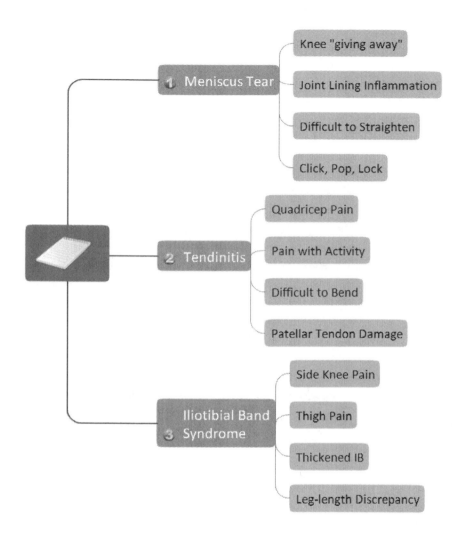

Moving on, for each symptom, we list qualifying questions as well as tests and tasks we need to perform to establish its existence. A common procedure to determine a click, pop, or locking of the knee is to perform the McMurry Test or an Arthroscopy. To determine if pain exists during physical activity, we can ask the patient to run, jump, kneel, and squat. To detect presence of a thickened or inflamed iliotibal band, the Ober's Test is performed. To determine existence of other symptoms, we perform stability, flexibility, range of motion, and tenderness tests on and around the knee or order MRIs, X-rays, and/or Ultrasound. Adding this information to the rest of the symptoms gives us a map like so:

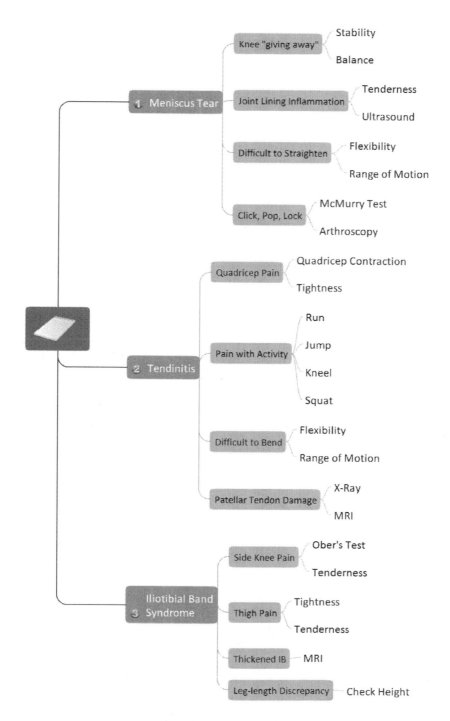

- **1 Meniscus Tear**
  - Knee "giving away"
    - Stability
    - Balance
  - Joint Lining Inflammation
    - Tenderness
    - Ultrasound
  - Difficult to Straighten
    - Flexibility
    - Range of Motion
  - Click, Pop, Lock
    - McMurry Test
    - Arthroscopy

- **2 Tendinitis**
  - Quadricep Pain
    - Quadricep Contraction
    - Tightness
  - Pain with Activity
    - Run
    - Jump
    - Kneel
    - Squat
  - Difficult to Bend
    - Flexibility
    - Range of Motion
  - Patellar Tendon Damage
    - X-Ray
    - MRI

- **3 Iliotibial Band Syndrome**
  - Side Knee Pain
    - Ober's Test
    - Tenderness
  - Thigh Pain
    - Tightness
    - Tenderness
  - Thickened IB
    - MRI
  - Leg-length Discrepancy
    - Check Height

Looking above, we have a thorough diagram of our diagnosis. In the first level, we listed the possible ailments causing the pain. In the second level, we added symptoms one should observe if that ailment existed. Within the third level, we included tests and actions that will confirm existence or nonexistence of each symptom. All the necessary information to make an accurate diagnosis is clearly laid out. At this stage, all that is needed is to perform the tests to determine the existence of the symptoms. The ailment with the most observed symptoms is likely the cause of the pain.

As stated in the beginning of the section, medicine is not the only area diagnosis can be used. It can be used any time you are trying to get to the root of a problem, whether it is with your plumbing or a broken television. So the next time a problem arises whose origin you can't identify, begin with a Mind Map.

Presentation

Once you have written, brainstormed, planned, problem solved, diagnosed, or done the many other things possible with Mind Maps, you may have to present the result. Just as you can take notes of a presentation or lecture with a Mind Map, you can also use it to prepare for and deliver one. Using a Mind Map to deliver a presentation allows you to make sure you cover all the ideas and information you want, but still are flexible and fresh in your delivery.

When you are preparing for your presentation, create a Mind Map for the presentation the same way you would for a research paper or other writing project. This will serve as your note card or outline, but without forcing you into a specific tempo or progression.

Before your presentation, go through the following steps:

1. Pick the order you will go over your subtopics.

2. Write an introductory sentence to get your presentation started.

3. Write intro sentences for each subtopic.

4. Make several copies of your Mind Map.

5. If you are using visual aids, label them.

   a. Note on your Mind Map which aid goes with which subset or subtopic.

   b. Organize your aids so you can access any of them when necessary.

6. Plan a concluding statement.

7. Practice your presentation using the copies.

When you give the presentation (or when you practice it), try this approach:

1. Introduce the main topic starting with your prepared sentence.

2. Introduce your first subtopic and go on to discuss it in detail.

3. As you cover each subset, check or cross it off.

4. Go through the subsets in the order that feels most comfortable.

5. Skim over things the audience isn't interested in or not responding to.

6. Spend extra time on ideas and subsets that the audience gets excited about.

7. When you have covered all the subsets in the first subtopic, move on to the next subtopic.

8. Repeat steps 2-7 for each subtopic.

9. Conclude your presentation.

After practicing several times, you will be comfortable with your presentation and probably will have worked out a general order of how to cover subsets, though you can vary that order if you want later.

Using Mind Maps for a presentation means you aren't doing the same presentation every time. You don't need to worry about sounding rehearsed or getting bored with your own work. Each presentation will be a little different, with a different emphasis and different details depending on your audience and your choices. This keeps your material fresh and enjoyable for you and your audience.

Recalling Information

Thus far we have talked a great deal about how mind maps improve memory. Mind Maps are useful not just for memory, but recall as well. You are probably wondering what the difference might be between memory and recall. In many respects, they are one and the same, but there is a slight difference.

The process of remembering a thought or idea has two parts. One is putting the information in your head. This involves taking something you want to learn and remember and driving it into your brain so that it is committed to *memory*. The other has to do with bringing the information out or *recalling* it. This deals with locating the information that now resides in your head and bringing it out into your awareness to use. Just because memory goes into your head, doesn't mean it will necessarily come out, come out easily, or come out when you need it most. This is what we refer to as *forgetting*.

For this reason, often you don't actually need help with memory. Instead, what you really need is help in recall. The information you seek is already in your head; either you actively committed it to memory or your natural processes took it in at some point. You just need a way to access it. You need to trace through your thoughts to find that information.

Mind Maps are great for recall for the same reasons they are for memory. Earlier in the book we talked about the power of association. We mentioned that by linking your thoughts, you have an easier time remembering them. We also mentioned that with its interconnecting neurons, your mind is built to do this naturally. In fact, it is doing it all the time with all of your thoughts and experiences. Since your brain is always building these connections, you can use mind maps to trace them and back track to previous thoughts and events and withdraw information from those moments.

So how does recall work? The process of recall is unique. It depends on the type of information you are trying to recall. Although unique, the general approach is to:

1. Write a question about what you want to remember in the middle of the page. By posing a question as the main topic, you trigger your mind to start thinking of answers and solutions. As you are building your map, the ideas you get for branches and sub-branches will be more consistent with leading you to an answer.

2. Think about facts and events that might help trigger memory of that information. Place these items around the center. It helps to think about material and events related to the subject or the location you heard or learned the information.

3.   From there, build connections and relationships. Trace these connections and relationships to other thoughts and ideas. Keep doing this until the answer is revealed.

We will walk you through two examples to illustrate how this works. One example will show you how to locate something you've lost, and the other will help you remember important facts. These examples will give you a framework of how to recall other types of information like directions and events.

Recalling Lost Items

For the first example, imagine you have a special bracelet that a dear friend gave to you. You wear it everywhere you go, as it keeps her close. In fact, you never leave home without it.

As you get home from a long and busy day, though, you notice that the bracelet is no longer on your wrist. You've lost the bracelet and are frantic about where it could be. To help recall where you may have left or lost it, you draw a Mind Map.

You start with the main topic, *Where is my Bracelet?* Notice that in this situation, we did not start with a statement like *bracelet* or *Joan's bracelet* as a main topic. Instead, we posed a question. This will trigger our mind to think in the background about where the bracelet might be.

Once you have the main topic down, think about all the places where you last remember seeing the bracelet, whether on your arm or elsewhere. For example, you remember seeing it on the bathroom sink because you put it there before hopping in the shower. You remember fiddling with it on your lunch break. You also remember it on your arm during your morning commute to work. For each place you recall having the bracelet, put it on the Mind Map as a subtopic or first level branch. Try to think of as many places as possible. The more locations you can come up with, the more links you can trace to find the answer.

Now, put an approximate date or time next to each location on the map. For example, you showered shortly after waking up in morning, so the time you saw the bracelet on the bathroom sink was approximately 6:30 a.m. You ate lunch between 12:00 and 1:00, so that is an estimate of when you saw it during your lunch break. You left for work at 8:00 a.m., so that is the time you remember the bracelet during the morning commute. Do this for all the locations. This will give you a mind map with a collection of subtopics listing all the places and times you last remember seeing the item.

From here, identify the branch that is the latest in the day. This will be the last location you remember the bracelet and the starting point for your search. You can eliminate all prior locations as possible searching points because the jewelry was still in your possession after these times. That is, if on your map you remember having the bracelet when going for coffee after work, that means you didn't lose it at home in the bathroom, during your commute in the morning, nor in the break room at lunch. Since it was in your possession after these events, you must have lost your friend's gift at a subsequent time and place.

To narrow in on the subsequent time or place, take the branch you identified as the last location, and with subset or second level branches, add everything you did or places you went from that moment. This will be the connection or link that you follow. After the coffee shop, you remember going to Panera Bread for a pre-dinner snack. Then you went to the post office to drop off a package. Afterwards you went to the gym to workout. Add these items to the coffee shop branch.

Now ask yourself if you remember having your keys at any of these times and places. You don't remember if you had the bracelet at Panera Bread. You may have had it there, but for the moment, the memory of it does not come to mind. You do have a memory of it at the post office because you remember it got caught on the side of the package you were handing to the attendant. However, you definitely don't remember having it at the gym. Since you remember having it at the post office, trying to determine whether you had the bracelet at Panera is irrelevant, since your visit there occurred prior to the post office. You now have narrowed in on a more precise time and location you could have lost the jewelry.

At this point you can do one of two things. One, you can repeat the previous step by taking the branch you last remember seeing the bracelet and trying to remember all the places you went from that point. For example, after the post office you went to your car. You drove and did not get out of the car until you arrived at the gym. You walked into the entrance of the gym and swiped in. You went to the locker room to change. Yes, you remember having the bracelet in the locker room because you were careful not to catch it on your sleeves as you were changing.

The other thing you can do is take the most recent location you don't remember seeing the bracelet and work backwards to recall everything you did prior to that point. You remember running on the treadmill with no recollection of the bracelet. So you work backwards from there. Before the treadmill, you were in the weight room. Prior to the weight room, you were stretching in the aerobics room. Prior to stretching, you were at the juice bar. You went there to buy a smoothie before your workout.

Eureka–that is where you left the bracelet! When you went to pay for the drink, the jewel slipped off your arm. You put it on the counter so you could free your hands to pay the cashier. After taking the change from the cashier, you forgot to pick it back up. You even see the whole event replay in your mind with visions of yourself putting the item down and then walking away.

You drive back to the gym, rush to the juice bar, and guess what? The bracelet is behind the counter. The cashier saw you leave it at the register, so she put it back there until you returned. This is how you can *recall* something you have forgotten or lost.

In this example, we were able to pinpoint the exact location of the bracelet. It is important to note, however, that this may not always be the case. Sometimes, you will be able to simply narrow in on several possibilities. For example, if you dropped your bracelet somewhere instead of leaving it at the smoothie counter, you will not have a memory of exactly where it fell. However, you still increase the likelihood of finding it because you have narrowed in on the possible places to look. You know you lost it in the gym, likely near the tread mill, weight room, or aerobic room. You have a clear recollection of the bracelet prior to these places, but not after. You can then go to these three areas and look around or ask the attendant there if he or she had seen it.

This is Mind Mapping for finding lost items. Now we will look at how to recall facts.

Recalling Facts

Henry is a junior high student taking a geography test. He comes across a question asking the name of the tallest waterfall in the world.

He doesn't remember learning about this waterfall, nor was it in the notes he reviewed last night. As a result, he has no idea what the name of this fall could be or even where it is located. However, he knows that if the question is being asked, it was likely discussed in class and that he probably learned it, so the answer is likely residing in his head somewhere. He just needs to trace through his thoughts to find it.

He believes the topic was addressed the day the teacher discussed the geography of South America, specifically Colombia, Peru, Brazil, and Venezuela. So he starts a Mind Map with these 4 countries as the main branches.

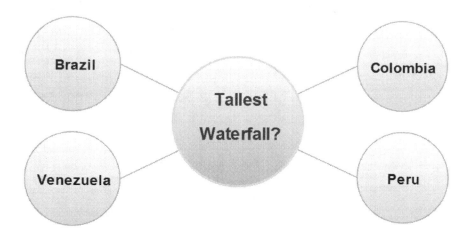

Note that the question doesn't ask the country the fall is in, but rather its name. Nonetheless, this is just a starting point for Henry. He is taking the situation where he may have learned this information and using memory of other facts he remembers learning to trace back to the answer.

He starts with Brazil and notes everything he remembers about the country. He records Rio de Janeiro as a major city of Brazil. He also notes that it is the largest South American country. Whatever comes to mind, he places it somewhere within the subtopic of Brazil. He also remembers that the country has several natural wonders, including the Amazon River and a major waterfall, which he notes as well.

He then does the same for Peru. He recalls the major cities are Lima and Cusco. Near Cusco is one of the seven wonders of the new world, Machu Picchu. Peru is also surrounded by desert, and within the desert is a famous oasis called Huacachina. He notes all this in the subtopic for Peru.

After continuing this for Colombia, his mind map looks as follows:

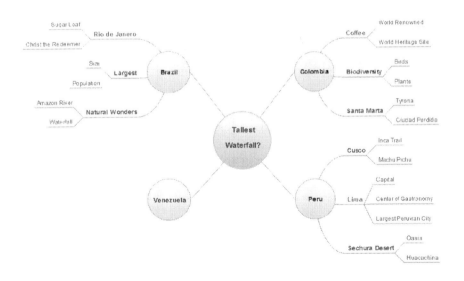

As you can see, he has filled in information for Brazil, Peru, and Colombia. Remember, he is simply writing down what comes to mind.

He then proceeds to Venezuela. He remembers the capital to be Caracas. He notes important information about Caracas and other facts that come to mind. He remember watching a travel channel special on the beaches of Los Roques off the coast of Venezuela. Although this isn't something his teacher discussed or he read in his text book, the information comes up and is related to the subtopic, so he writes it down. It might lead him to the answer.

Although it doesn't lead him to the answer directly, it does lead him to thinking about another Venezuelan island destination called Margarita, which he remembers his teacher talking about. Afterwards, the discussion of a waterfall comes up. Then all of a sudden his thoughts switch to the *Los Angeles Angels*, the major league baseball team. In that moment, he realizes the name of the waterfall, *Angel Falls*. When his teacher said *angel*, his mind drifted to thinking about the baseball team with the same name, and that is why he failed to remember or write this fact in his notes.

Now he has narrowed in on a waterfall and its name—*Angel*. He is quite positive this is his answer, though he wants to make sure because he also came up with a waterfall in Brazil.

He goes back to the subtopic Brazil on his Mind Map. He realizes he hasn't come up with the name of that waterfall. Right now that doesn't matter, as his goal is to figure out whether it or Angel falls is the tallest. He remembers seeing a picture of the Brazilian falls in his textbook. Although it was very large and wide, he doesn't remember it being so tall.

Based on this, he concludes that the answer is likely *Angel Falls*. He doesn't remember any discussion of waterfalls in Colombia nor Peru. Although a recollection of a falls came up in Brazil, he is certain it is not the tallest. He is sure of a discussion of a waterfall in Venezuela and is sure of the name, so this is likely his answer. This is another way to use Mind Maps for recall.

In this scenario, we began with countries as subtopics, but you could begin any number of ways. You may know all the major waterfalls of the world like *Niagara*, *Angel*, *Iguazu*, *Kaietur*, and *Victoria*. You just don't know which one is the tallest. You can start with these as subtopics. From here, you identify as many features of these waterfalls as possible. You keep identifying the features until somewhere a sub-branch shows up that leads you to the memory of the one that is the tallest.

In another scenario, you may know for a fact the fall resides in Venezuela, but it's just the name you are missing. You could start the recall process by placing Venezuela in the center. Then begin listing the names of places in the country you do remember. From there, you create links and connections to the names of other places until the name of the fall is revealed.

Creating a Mind Map like this can be a great strategy when taking exams. Not only will it help you recall answers you have difficulty remembering, but it will place on paper knowledge that may be helpful in answering other questions. For example, if on the same exam Henry is asked about the capital of Peru, he can quickly refer to the map and answer *Lima* because he has it written on his map. He may even be able to reference the map to answer essay questions.

As Henry proceeds with the exam, he can continually build and expand the map to get more and more of his knowledge out on to paper. This way, at the end of the exam, when he goes back to review his answers, he will have a detailed mind map to reference.

These are some suggestions to help you recall the information residing in your head that don't want to come out in the moment you want them. Since Mind Maps are structured similar to the brain, they allow you to follow a thought or event as the brain recorded it. If your brain has stored an event using various associations, you can gain access to it by recreating those associations using a mind map. You create branches and sub-branches that help you trace back to the event. This gives you the ability to locate lost and forgotten memories more accurately.

Recall is one of those areas that work best with Mind Mapping. You can try following your thoughts in your head, but often there are too many possibilities to work through. Usually everything gets jumbled together, causing you to lose track of what moment happened at what time and in what place. This can cloud your perception and create a sense of hopelessness. Traditional notes and outlines don't work either because they don't allow you to associate your thinking, which is essential to triggering related memories. This is one of the reasons you don't hear much about recall as a memory technique. Mind Mapping is a unique tool that can bring out the power of recall to aid memory.

Learning a Language

If you have ever had to learn a foreign language, you know that it is no walk in the park. It takes months to years to build a basic understanding of a language and even longer to become fluent. During the process, you may mix up definitions and expressions, causing you to say things you do not mean or make meaning of things that were not said. At times it can leave you speechless as you try to search your mental filing cabinet for the correct terms to use and in the correct order.

Mind Mapping is one of the best kept secrets in learning a foreign language. Its design puts structure and order to everything you are learning so you can absorb more information more easily. With Mind Maps, you can drastically reduce the time and effort needed to acquire a new or second language. In this section, you will see just how easy it can be.

In order to provide meaningful instructions and illustrations, we will use a real world example of learning to speak Spanish. You can carry the instructions over to other languages. Since every language is unique, you may not be able to carry over ideas exactly. Nonetheless, you will get a general sense of how the technique can be applied in this area.

Building Vocabulary

The best place to start when learning a language is building vocabulary. An extensive vocabulary is the cornerstone of speaking and understanding a dialect. The more words you know, the more words you can use to communicate and the more words you can understand in another person's communication.

The difficulty with vocabulary is that you have to learn the definitions of hundreds to thousands of words. With such quantity, everything can easily get mixed up. You may recognize a word, but not know the translation, or you may know the translation, but it may not come up fast enough to use. You may also confuse the translation with a completely unrelated word. Looking at the words *cat* and *car*, you will notice both look almost identical, though changing one letter changes the meaning completely.

Mind Maps help by organizing all the words you are learning. You don't learn words individually in list form and without relation to a higher context. Instead, you categorize vocabulary so you learn them in relation to each other and within the framework of other words. For example, if you are going to learn vocabulary of items around the house, you can set up a mind map like so:

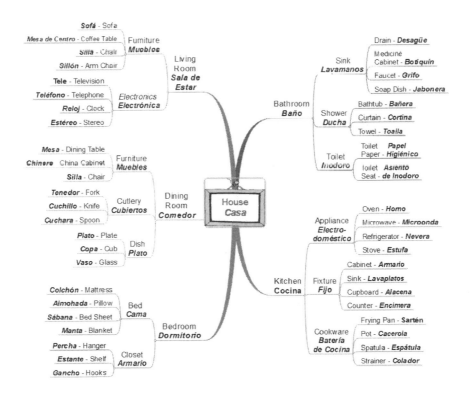

Here is another example:

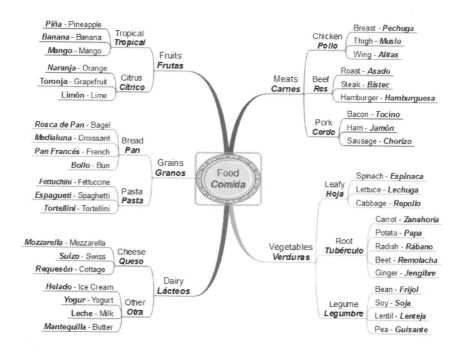

This is an easier and more efficient way to build your vocabulary. Not only is all the information organized and grouped together, but everything is interconnected. If you can recall the translation of a word such as *apple*, you need move only a few branches to remember the translation of other words around it like *orange*, *melon*, or even *tomato*. If you encounter a word whose translation you do not remember, but can recognize the branch from where it came, you can still understand the context in which it is being used.

This is in contrast to studying a list of random words. First, such a list is very intimidating to approach. Imagine opening a dictionary and trying to memorize all the words on a page. The mere thought is enough to make you cringe. Also, there is no way to associate the words or definitions to other ideas. As a result, you will have random translations floating in your head with no real way to make them stick in your mind. When trying to recall a word, you couldn't use the power of association to help you.

Language learning is one area where pictures can be instrumental. Instead of putting the definition in English, you can use a picture. So instead of using the words *orange*, *mango*, *banana*, you replace them with their corresponding images. The visual component will make it easier to connect the words to their translations.

You can build vocabulary Mind Maps like this with all types of words. You can create a date and time mind map with first-level branches for *Days*, *Months*, and *Seasons*. Then list the names of the each of the days, months, and seasons with their translations under the appropriate subtopic. To learn the parts of the body, you can create a human anatomy Mind Map with *Arm*, *Leg*, *Body*, *Head*, and *Face* as the first-level branches. From here, you list the parts that belong under each appendage. You would list finger, nail, thumb, knuckles under *Arm*; eyes, nose, mouth, ears under *Face;* and so on. With this approach, you can learn thousands of words and phrases far more quickly than with traditional methods.

One of the most difficult aspects of learning a foreign language is keeping all the rules of grammar, spelling, pronunciation, and conjugation straight in your head. That is, the difficulty with learning a language does not end with having to remember the many rules of grammar, spelling, etc. You also have to make sure not to confuse the rules with each other. This involves selecting the correct words and applying them in the correct way and in the correct context.

Nowhere is this difficulty more prevalent than with pronouns. A pronoun is a word that stands in for or represents a noun. There are many types of pronouns. There is the subjective pronoun—*I, you, he, she, we,* and *they.* There is also the possessive pronoun—*mine, yours, his, hers, ours,* and *theirs.* There are direct object pronouns—*me, you, him, her, us,* and *them.* There are also indirect object pronouns—*to me, to you, to him, to us,* and *to them.* These are some examples of pronouns.

Native speakers of English are so accustomed to talking in the language that they don't think about these distinctions. In fact, many of us have probably never heard of what a pronoun is or are even conscious of using it when writing or speaking. Nonetheless, when learning a new language, this is very important. It can make the difference between saying *I like his bag* to *me like him bag.* I am sure you agree the latter sounds ridiculous.

Mind Maps can help prevent this type of confusion. As mentioned, the system puts structure and organization in your learning. This structure allows you to keep related rules and concepts together, while still allowing you to see the differences between them. Not only can you see that a distinction exists, but Mind Mapping keeps you from mixing them up. This way you don't confuse one set of rules with another.

You can create a Mind Map that makes the distinction between the various pronouns apparent as follows.

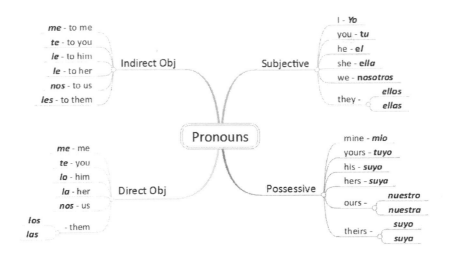

In the above map, one set of branches lists subjective pronouns, another lists possessive, and the other two, direct and indirect. These aren't the only pronouns in

Spanish. There are others, such as the reflexive–*myself*, *yourself*, *him/herself*, *ourselves*, and *themselves*. Each time you learn a new pronoun type, you can add it to the map so you are aware of the variations and how to apply them correctly.

Another area that creates confusion is in learning demonstrative adjectives like *the*, *this*, and *that*. Spanish puts a lot of emphasis on gender, so adjectives must agree in gender with the word they are describing. Adjectives must also agree in number. For example, in Spanish, the word glass (vaso) is a masculine word. To say *the* glass, you say *el* vaso. The word cup (copa) in Spanish is feminine. To say *the* cup, one says *la* copa. In the plural form, *the* glasses becomes *los* vasos and the cup becomes *las* copas. As you can see, the word *the* has four translations in Spainsh—*el*, *la*, *los*, *las*.

The same goes for the adjectives *this* and *that*. The translations for *this* are *este*, *esta*, *estos*, and *estas*. The translations for *that* include *ese*, *esa*, *esos*, and *esas*. As mentioned, the version you use depends on whether the word it is describing is masculine or feminine and singular or plural. So any time you want to use one of these words, you have to pick from four variations.

It is easy to see how confusing this can be. Not only do you have to remember 4 alternatives of each word, but you have to make sure not to mix up the alternatives with each other. One can easily mistake *esos*, the masculine plural of *that,* with *esta,* the feminine singular of *this.* However, a mind map can make this distinction very clear and apparent.

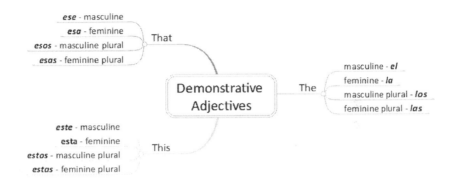

In the above Mind Map, we have a separate branch for *the*, *this*, and *that*, which lists the related translations. This diagram makes it evident that four distinctions of each word exist and what those distinctions are. This way it is easier to pick the correct translation for use in the correct context. If you wanted, you could make the distinction more evident by creating a mind map like so.

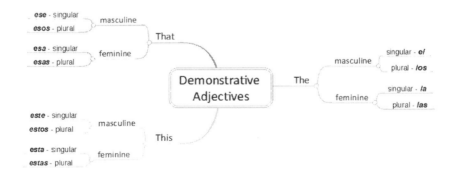

Looking above, the first-level branches list the adjectives. The second level separates out into choices for masculine and feminine. The third level separates each masculine and feminine branch into choices for singular or plural, where the translations are noted. This is a nice way to separate the variations. If we wanted to say *that cat*, we would start with the light blue branch labeled *That*. *Cat* is a masculine word, so we follow the branch labeled *masculine*. The word is singular, so we follow that branch to get the definition *ese*, to say *ese gato* or *that cat*.

Like pronouns, there are many forms of adjectives. There are the demonstrative adjectives that we learned here. There are also possessive, interrogative, and adjectives of number and quantity. Like the pronouns Mind Map, we can create a Mind Map for adjectives that lists out and defines all the varieties.

Mastering Verbs

Another area where Mind Maps prove useful is in learning to conjugate verbs. Verbs are words that express action (walk, run, dance, eat) or state of being (is, am, are). In order to use a verb in a sentence, it first needs to be modified or conjugated. One of the most difficult aspects of Spanish is learning to conjugate verbs correctly. This is because verb conjugation is much more different and complex in Spanish.

For starters, in Spanish, the verb endings change depending on which person or subject – *I*, *you*, *he/she*, *we*, or *they* – is performing the action. To illustrate what we mean, let's look at the conjugation of the verb *to dance* in both languages. The Spanish translation for dance is *bailar*. The two sets of conjugations are noted in the table below.

To Dance	Bailar
I dance	Yo Bail**o**
You dance	Tu Bail**as**
He/She dances	El/Ella Bail**a**
We dance	Nosotros Bail**amos**
They dance	Ellos/Ellas Bail**an**

In English, this verb conjugates with the different subjects as follows: I *dance*, you *dance*, he/she *dances*, we *dance*, and they *dance*. If you notice, there is no variation in the *I*, *you*, *we* and *they* forms of the conjugation. The variation exists only in the *he/she* form, where the verb changes from *dance* to *dances*, as in he *dances* or she *dances*.

This is in direct contrast to Spanish. In Spanish, the verb ending changes based on the person performing the action. If you look at the above table again, for this particular verb, the *ar* at the end of the word is dropped to form the stem *bail*. Then depending on the subject, one of the following is added to the stem: *o*, *as*, *a*, *amos*, or *an*. If the subject is *I*, -*o* is added to form *bailo*. If the subject is *you*, instead of *-o*, *-as* is added to form *bailas*. For *he/she*, *we*, and *they*, *-a*, *-amos*, or *–an* are added respectively to form either *baila*, *bailamos*, and *bailan*. This is one reason that makes Spanish verb conjugation difficult.

Another reason is that ending rules change depending on the verb type. Spanish has three types of verbs— verbs that end in *ar*, *er*, and *ir*. As you learned, the rule for *ar* verbs, such as *bailar*, is to first drop the *–ar*. Then based on the subject, add the following to the stem: *o*, *as*, *a*, *amos*, or *an*. The rule for *Er* verbs is to drop the *–er*, and add a different set of endings: *o*, *es*, *e*, *emos*, or *en*. *Ir* verbs drop the *–ir* and add a set of ending similar to Er verbs: *o*, *es*, *e*, *imos*, or *en*. So to correctly conjugate a verb in Spanish, one has to not only take into account the subject—*I*, *you*, *he/she*, *we*, and *they*— but the verb type—*ar*, *er*, and *ir*—as well.

At initial glance, remembering and applying these rules seems confusing and difficult. With a Mind Map, however, it is quite simple. First, we start with the 3 verb types as first-level branches.

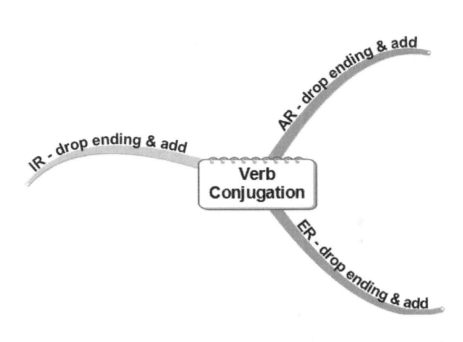

Then we list the subjects around each type as second-level branches.

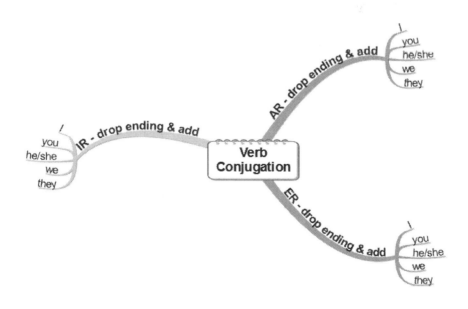

From here, we place the ending to be applied to each subject.

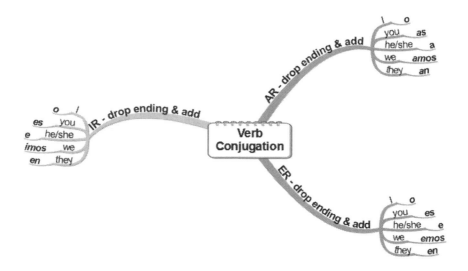

To use this map, let's say I want to use the verb *comer*, which means *to eat*, in a sentence. More specifically, I want to say *John eats*. To conjugate the verb, I first look at the verb ending. This verb ends in *er*, so I start with the green branch on the map. The action is performed by John, so I reference the sub-branch for *he*. This sub-branch instructs us to drop the *–er* ending and add *e* to the stem. Dropping the *-er* in *comer* gives me the stem *com*. Adding *e* forms *come*. I insert *John* in front of *come* to form *John come* which translates to *John eats*.

See how easy Mind Maps make learning to conjugate verbs? They have taken an intricate set of rules and conventions and simplified it. One can use this Mind

Map to conjugate any regular Spanish verb in the present tense.

Unfortunately, the difficulty with verb conjugation doesn't end here. It gets more complicated when dealing with tenses. Tense refers to the time a verb's action occurs. So far we have dealt with a verb's action in the present tense, as in *I dance* or *I eat*. A verb's action can occur in the past as in *I danced* or *I ate*. It occurs in the imperfect as in *I was dancing* or *I was eating*. It also occurs in the future such as *I will dance* or *I will eat*. Finally, there is the conditional such as *I would dance* or *I would eat*. These are the 5 main tenses in Spanish (there are more, but these are the principal ones that we will focus our discussion around).

For the most part, dealing with tenses in English is fairly straight forward. Depending on the tense, you make minor modifications like adding *was*, *will*, or *would* before the verb. In Spanish, this is not so.

Spanish uses a unique set of endings for each verb tense. The endings used to express action in the present tense differ from ones used to express action in the past or future tenses. This means that when conjugating a verb, the ending you use depends not only on the subject and verb type, but the tense of the verb action as well. Therefore, any time you want to conjugate a verb, you have to choose from approximately 75 different verb endings (5 subjects x 3 verb types x 5 tenses). Talk about overwhelming.

Again, with Mind Maps, there is no need to feel overwhelmed. To incorporate the additional rules required to conjugate verbs by their tense, we simply add another layer to the Mind Map we created above.

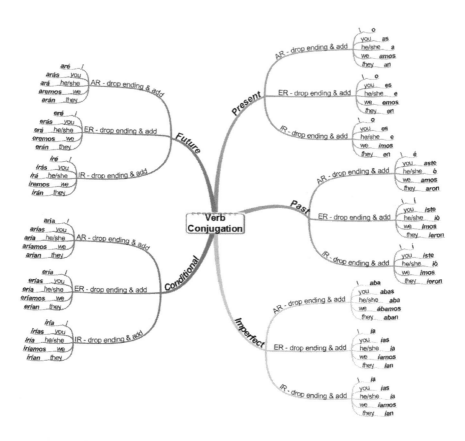

This mind map begins the first-level branches with the 5 tenses—present, past, imperfect, future, and conditional. Then it adds the 3 verb types *ar*, *er*, and *ir* to each tense as second-level branches. From there, third-level branches are added with the subjects. Finally, next to each subject, the ending to use is listed. In a simple format, this mind map lists all the rules needed to conjugate a regular Spanish verb, irrespective of subject, type, or tense.

Putting it all Together

Now that you have learned the various ways to apply mind maps for language learning, let's put everything together. Say we want to translate the following sentence into Spanish: *They will open that window*. First we translate the subject *they*. We go to the pronoun mind map and choose the branch labeled *subject*. The subject branch translates *they* as *ellos*.

Next we translate the verb. The sentence says *will open*, which is the future tense. So we start with the blue branch labeled *future*. The verb to open is *abrir*. Looking at the ending, we notice this is an *ir* verb, so we select the branch for this verb type. The form we are looking for is *they*. The branch says to drop -*ir* and add *iran*. Doing so gives us *abriran*. Combining *ellos* with *abriran* forms *ellos abriran*, which means *they will open*. This translates the first half of the sentence.

To translate the remaining half, *that window*, we go to the vocabulary Mind Map to find that *window* is *ventana*. Pretty simple. Now we need to select the correct form of *that*. If you remember, in Spanish *that* has 4 translations, so we go to the adjective Mind Map to locate the correct one. Ventana is a feminine word, so we follow the corresponding branch. We are using the singular form, which is *esa*.   Combining the four translations together gives us *ellos abriran esa ventanta—they will open that window.*

How wonderful! In a few pages of text and with a few simple Mind Maps, you now have a basic understanding of Spanish.   Obviously, there are more rules and intricacies to the language, but this is a good beginning. You can use these illustrations as a model to learn other words and rules to further enhance your understanding and fluency.

CHAPTER SIX – MIND MAPPING WITH CHILDREN

With more and more people discovering and using Mind Maps, there is a movement among educators familiar with the technique to try to apply it to educating children.

Michael Tipper, a speed-reading instructor and teacher of Mind Mapping to children, says that the approach of the teacher should be based on the age and maturity of the student, for a child who is too young or not mature enough will be bored by Mind Mapping and will not be able to grasp the process.

Tipper himself does not inform the children he is tutoring that they are going to learn about Mind Mapping *per* se. Rather, he tells the children that they will be learning about a particular subject that is easy for them to grasp—say, a farm. He will use a very large piece of paper, then ask the children to draw a picture of a farm. This picture of a farm acts as the Mind Map's key central idea.

Tipper then asks the children to name the things which they think belong on a farm. He makes it a point to encourage the children to use generic words to label those things such as Machinery, Barns, Fences, Animals and the like. Tipper draws lines from the key central idea—Farm—on which he gets the children to draw the images of the things that belong on a farm. These things make up the keywords of subtopics.

Under each subtopic, Tipper will then draw more lines to reflect the supporting details. He will then pull the children further into the Mind Mapping process by asking them leading questions. As an example, for a subtopic dubbed *Animals*, Tipper would ask the children what kind of animals can be found on a farm. The children might say *Chickens, Sheep, Pigs, Cows, Horses* and so on and so forth.

It might look something like this.

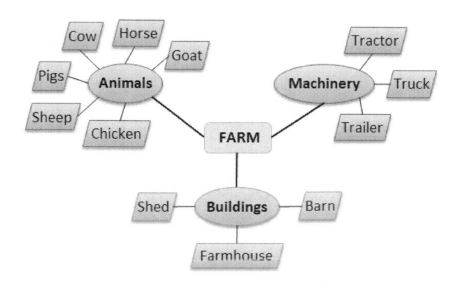

He would then ask the children again either to draw images of such animals or to look for pictures in magazines. Tipper notes that children do not usually follow the logical approach of Mind Mapping that is geared for adults. The diagram that results from Tipper's approach to teaching children is one that is composed mainly of pictures. This is appropriate for encouraging children to become creative and spontaneous.

Tipper discourages linear approaches to teaching children since their ability to express themselves may be stifled. Tipper's approach is also useful for encouraging children to work in groups—one group could be responsible for one branch of information while the other groups work on the different branches.

The advantage of using this method when teaching children is that this way makes sense to them. More importantly, it makes it more fun to go through lessons. After a Mind Mapping session, ask one of the participating children what the lesson was about, and the child will then think of the illustration that was created and be able to describe to you in his or her own words what the teacher taught that day. If the children who participate in the process are just learning how to read, the teacher could paste on the Mind Map the names of the things in the pictures using large letters. The children would then be able to relate the picture to the word pasted beside it.

CHAPTER SEVEN – OTHER CONSIDERATIONS

The Importance of Practice

At the start, this technique requires practice. Though those who master the art of Mind Mapping eventually find that more information is absorbed and recalled in proportion to the effort required to learn it.

Buzan advocates that people trying out Mind Mapping should do up to 100 Mind Maps before they can become comfortable with the tool—whether it is applied for note-taking, planning, organizing, or simply jotting down one's thoughts and feelings. One persistent user believes that it is advantageous to create at least one Mind Map every month regularly. He feels that Mind Mappers will eventually want to use larger and larger pieces of paper as the relationships between their ideas expand.

The Importance of Listening

Bad listening habits are observed by people around us on a daily basis—and even we may be guilty of practicing them as well. When we listen to a speaker, do we often reject the subject at hand as being not interesting enough? Or do we pass judgment on the speaker based on his mannerisms or delivery, thus not paying attention to the content of his speech?

On the other hand, we might become too carried away by the topic of the speech and fail to be critical listeners. Do we listen mainly for facts, or do we predominantly look for testimonials or even entertainment instead? Do we attempt to outline the entire content of the speech? Are we just pretending to pay attention to the speaker? Do we permit distractions to prevent us from listening? Do we dodge difficult portions of the speech? Do highly emotional trigger words have the ability to agitate us to the point that we become very hostile? Or do we just daydream throughout the speech, wasting both our time and that of the speaker's?

Bad habits such as these prevent us from taking advantage of someone's efforts to communicate to us. These habits are also responsible for creating terrible Mind Maps. How can you create a map that makes sense to you if you are not able to grasp the flow of a speaker's ideas? How can you know where one idea links up with another to form a certain relationship if you fail to listen well? And if you do not know how to listen well, how can you learn to communicate the same ideas to other people when they ask you about it?

A Mind Map is only as good as the creator's ability to form relationships between concepts. To understand relationships between concepts, you have to listen closely and notice where one relationship ends and another begins. To become a good speaker yourself, you must first be able to listen to how the presenter imparted his ideas then attempt to replicate the process. Part of replicating that process is creating a good Mind Map on which you can base your own presentation.

The ARCURRC Model of Listening

Buzan outlines the steps of the listening process in his ARCURRC model. Looking through the model allows you to zero in on any of the steps where you may be deficient or experiencing problems. This way, you can attempt to improve your listening habits. The ARCURRC model is broken down into seven steps: Assimilation, Recognition, Comprehension, Understanding, Retention, Recall, and Communication (or Use).

Assimilation deals with the functioning of your ears and brain to hear and grasp the sounds in your environment. If you feel that you might have a problem with assimilation, it might help to undergo a thorough hearing exam to rule out problems with your hearing. Even people confident about their ability to hear may find it beneficial to have such an exam done. This way you will know without a doubt if your hearing is at a normal level—and if you can surpass that level.

Recognition deals with the capacity of your mind to decode sound waves received by your ears. It helps you identify from where a sound is emitted, such as words coming from a person, music coming from a radio, or the sound of an engine being revved up. Recognition is something we develop quite quickly in early childhood, but fail to practice as we grow up because we tend to tune out background sounds. You can advance your power of recognition if you continue to identify the source and nuances of different sounds in and around your environment—practice makes perfect.

Comprehension is the ability of your mind to interpret the information it is fed. Some people might have a problem with the internal structures connecting their hearing apparatus to their brain, which may explain why they find it hard to comprehend sounds and their meaning. It could also be traced to a problem within the brain itself. This would require a diagnosis by a doctor.

Understanding has to do with your mind's ability to form a relationship between information that has undergone assimilation, recognition, and comprehension to information already residing in memory. Good listeners continuously try to stay alert about their level of understanding and improve on this skill.

Retention is the capacity of your brain to keep previously-heard knowledge in memory. If you find it hard to retain information, you might want to work on your capacity to understand. This involves structuring and restructuring concepts as they are communicated to you. In the end, you will find that it is easier to retain information that you understand.

Recall also relates to memory. As you learned, it represents the ability of your mind to pull out information already in memory. You can improve recall by structuring ideas in better ways as you absorb them, just as when you want to improve retention.

The last phase of the listening process is Communication or Use. In this stage, the information which you have assimilated, recognized, comprehended, understood, and retained is then recalled in order to transfer your own message to other people. You communicate with other people through either spoken, written, or representational means. If you want to talk to yourself—yes, this is also communication—you simply think. A good listener can eventually become a good communicator to other people as well.

As we said before, it is important to have good listening skills if you want to produce useful Mind Maps. A good listener is able to absorb the content of a speaker's message more effectively and can comprehend such ideas better. A good listener can to do this because he or she hears how the different ideas are interrelated to one another based on the speaker's presentation and on how he connects the speaker's ideas to the knowledge in his own memory. The Mind Map that results from his or her efforts will make more sense not only to the person creating it, but also to other people who may look at it.

Speed Reading and Mind Maps

You may be wondering what speed reading has to do with Mind Mapping. Well, to start, both require the simultaneous use of your eyes and your mind. More importantly, speed reading will aid you in the mapping process. You will be able to absorb information at a faster rate, and then you can use Mind Mapping as a complement to what you have read. That's how it works.

Now, reading fast does not necessarily mean you are speed-reading. You might be reading fast, but not absorbing the information; your eyes are simply darting through the text, but nothing is entering your head. Genuine speed reading means that you are moving along swiftly while picking up the meaning along the way. In this section, we will present a powerful technique to help you achieve this. You will be able to pick up words quicker and understand them better.

Before presenting the technique, it helps to go back to our discussion of how our eyes and mind process information. If you recall, in the beginning of the book we shared that our mind recognizes a person's face as a whole, not in individual parts. It identifies a person not by looking at individual features such as the nose, mouth, ears etc. Instead, it develops an understanding by looking at the complete picture.

Now, what would happen if your eyes didn't look at the complete picture? What if you focused your sight on an individual feature of your friend, such as an eye lash, nostril, or dimple? Narrowing the focus of your vision on such a small detail would prevent you from seeing everything else. With a narrow focus like this, you would have to scan every part of the face individually to recognize the person's face.

This is the problem with reading. When people read, they narrow their focus to one word or even one letter. As a result, when they read, they have to advance part by part—letter to letter or word to word—to pick up any significant meaning. If they get distracted or their mind wanders to another thought, they miss the meaning of the entire sentence or paragraph and have to start over.

The solution is to not to focus your sight on individual words and letters. Instead, expand your visual awareness and look at chunks of words at a time. As stated several times, this is the natural way your mind processes information.

How does one expand visual awareness when reading? The best way to do this is not to look at the words, but rather at the spaces in between the words. You are probably wondering how looking at the spaces between words can help improve reading speed and comprehension. It helps because paying attention to the spaces keeps your eyes from getting too focused and fixated on individual words; as a result, they can pick up more information, for instance when recognizing a person's face.

We can spend hours explaining the whys and hows of this, with studies to back up the claim; however, it will be much easier to show you. Below is a two-sentence paragraph with a small dot in between each word. Go through the paragraph while glancing through each of the dots. Start with the first, then move to the second, then the third, and so on. When doing this, don't look at the words and don't try to verbalize what it says. Simply scan your eyes from one dot to the next with a quick pace.

Even • though • you • are • not • looking • at • any • of • the • words • in • this • paragraph • your • eyes • and • mind • are • still • able • to • pick • up • the • text. • This • happens • because • paying • attention • to • the • spaces • prevents • your • eyes • from • narrowing • their • focus.

Amazing, right? By paying attention to only the dots— the spaces between the words—your mind was able to capture the text rapidly. As a result, you were able to read more, at a faster speed, and with higher comprehension. If you were not able to pick up the text, go back to this exercise again. Remember, simply look at the dots in between the words in the above paragraph and move from one dot to the next swiftly.

This is the essence of speed reading. You grab text as a whole instead of its individual parts. When using this technique, don't analyze, evaluate, or verbalize the text, either out loud or in your head. Simply skim across the sentence from one blank space to the next without stopping or trying to make sure you understand what is being said. Just move your eyes from right to left in a steady rhythm. That is all you have to do. Just as when you are looking at a tree, a car, or anything else in your environment, your mind will pick up the information without your needing to think much about it.

Then to read faster, you transition from looking at the spaces between every word to looking at the spaces between every two words, and then every three words. With enough practice, you can progress to a stage where you can look at only a few spaces per line of text to grasp the information in that line quickly and with higher attention and comprehension.

However, don't immediately jump to this level. Practice first with a space between every word. Once you are comfortable, move up to glancing at spaces between every two words. Go up to a space every three words only once you are proficient with two. Eventually, as mentioned in the previous paragraph, you will progress to a point where you can absorb an entire sentence by glancing merely at two spaces, one in the middle-left and then to the middle-right.

Some people advance to the point that they glance at only one space—the one in the middle of the sentence—to capture its words. They can read through a paragraph or page of text by moving from one line of text down to the next while gazing only at the space in the middle of each line. With practice, you can achieve this as well.

The great thing about this technique is that it is not a skill you need to learn or develop. It is an innate ability that you and everyone already possess. It is the natural way your eyes and mind work to process information. Therefore, you need only to change your habit from looking at the words to the spaces between the words.

To ingrain this habit, practice this with all types of material you have to read. In the beginning, don't try to force yourself to comprehend what you are reading. Simply emphasize creating a habit of looking at the spaces. As mentioned, understanding and comprehension will come naturally, as when your eyes notice a friend.

Hand Drawn vs. Computerized Mind Maps

As touched on briefly in chapter 3, you can create a Mind Map using plain paper and various colored pens or you can opt to use one of the numerous types of computer mapping software that are out on the market. Some people might find it easier to take linear notes at the start, then translate these notes into Mind Maps later on.

This boils down to personal preferences. Many swear by hand-drawn Mind Maps, while others believe computerized versions made with the help of specialized software are better. One user engaged in business still likes to draw them by hand, but opts for the computer software version when he has to create diagrams that will be shared with other people or have to be continuously amended and updated over time.

Tony Buzan himself at first did not consider most Mind Mapping software out in the market to be part of the technique—he devoted himself to its application for learning (such as for studying in college). Now, though, he has also come out with his own personal software— the iMindMap program.

Computer software does have many benefits for people. One is that the map can be quite large if you wish. On paper, you are limited by the size of the sheet. Also, most software comes with an array of pre-set symbols (as opposed to you inventing symbols of your own). You can also change the organization of your branches even after it has been drawn. Web or desktop files can be linked to map nodes. You can email the map to other people or simply post it on your website. There are templates available now which you could use if you don't want to start from scratch. A Mind Map made with software can feature as high a level of detail as you wish. If you create a large map, you can search it. With all these advantages, the popularity of mapping software has definitely risen—one estimate is that 60,000 people per month try them.

Tony Buzan markets his own software product as the one program that can duplicate the effectiveness of the traditional hand-drawn Mind Maps. Its key features (according to Buzan) are unlimited visual variety, portability, freedom, brain friendliness, and effectiveness.

As it relates to cost, Mind Map software has a wide price range. Some programs are inexpensive, while others are quite costly. Some require a one-time purchase, while others require a yearly subscription. Still there are many that are absolutely free.

Now, paying more doesn't necessarily mean getting more. Some expensive programs offer little in terms of features and support. On the other hand, many free programs offer more choices and options and better design. With that said, there is really no need to buy expensive Mind Mapping software when so many free ones are readily available. Below are recommendations for some free software we enjoy using.

Edraw - http://www.edrawsoft.com/download-mindmap.php

Edraw is one of our favorite Mind Mapping software. It is easy to use with many pre-drawn templates and more than 600 symbols and samples. This allows you to create high-quality, professional-looking diagrams with little effort. Like any software, it requires a little getting used to.

Freeplane - http://freeplane.sourceforge.net/

Freeplane is another great solution. Although the end Mind Map you create is not as visually appealing as in Edraw, it is an easy and intuitive program with lots of flexibility.

Text2MindMap - http://www.text2mindmap.com/

If you want to avoid the hassle of installing third party files on your computer, an alternative is to use a web-based program. Text2MindMap does not require its user to download or install a software. It is an online tool that lets you quickly and easily create mind maps using a web browser. You navigate to the website, enter keywords in the textbox on the left, and the inserted text is converted in real time into a mind map on the right. This is the quickest way to get started using mind mapping software.

MindMapfree - http://mindmapfree.com/

MindMapfree is another online tool that allows you to easily create mind maps. It is very simple to use and gives you more flexibility in the creation and ordering of branches.

These are a few of the many software options for mind maps. The best feature of the above assortment is that they are free—no trial, purchase, or subscription required.

To discover additional software, Wikipedia has a list of over 40 programs, many of which are also free. The link to the list is:

http://en.wikipedia.org/wiki/List_of_Mind_Mapping_software

You can also download and try many different kinds of Mind Map software at www.download.com. Just type in *Mind Maps* in the search field. Some of these software packages are free to use, while others are for purchase, but still allow you to try them for free before buying.

CONCLUSION

Mind Mapping is an exciting tool that can be helpful to everyone, no matter what their situation. Even though it does take some time and energy initially to become comfortable using it, you will find that it is well worth the effort because it can become a great time-saver in the long run. Its many advantages and uses are not limited to what we have discovered in this book—each person, using their creativity and imagination, can come up with new and interesting ways to apply it.

You can use it instead of traditional note-taking entirely if that is your choice, but remember that there are no hard and fast rules, just guidelines that you can adapt to your own particular needs. You can switch from one method to another at will or combine them in whatever way is right for you.

If you took the time to read this book, it's likely that you have plenty in your life to remember and organize. This means you don't have the time to read, practice, and learn about a vastly new system of note taking and organization. As a result, the goal of this book was to be a fun and relaxed read. It was to present content in such a way that it seemed very intuitive and common sense. This way you are not wasting time trying to understand the information and how to use it. Instead, you can begin using it right away in your day-to-day life.

A more important goal with this version was to give you a wider range of uses. Most discussion of Mind Mapping revolves around using it primarily for note taking, studying, and brainstorming. As you learned here, Mind Maps do much more. They are a flexible and robust tool that can tackle a variety of problems, issues, and activities. The goal was to highlight these uses and with real word examples and applications.

So just because this book is an easy read with real world applications doesn't mean it was easy to put together. It took quite a bit of effort to go back and forth talking to readers and reviewers and incorporating their suggestions. It also took effort putting together the right set of graphics and illustrations to explain the concepts intuitively. So I hope you enjoyed the information and its ease of presentation. If you did, I would appreciate it if you can post a positive review of this book on Amazon.com or whichever site you made this purchase. It will encourage others to take a chance on this technique, which can help them lighten their mental load.

It's up to you now to apply the technique. Have fun with it!

* * *

Recommend Reading

With the success of this book, it is clear just how important Mind Maps are to people. As a result, for quite some time, I have been thinking about putting together a more advanced text. Fortunately, another author has done an exceptional job of this already. Instead of recreating the wheel, I'd like to recommend his book if you'd like to explore Mind Maps further. It goes deeper into the topic than any other work out there.

Although there will be some overlap with topics discussed here, you'll find his book approaches them from a different angle. The different perspective will help open your mind to the technique's many possibilities. More importantly, it contains many uses and topics not covered here including group Mind Mapping, a heavy discussion of other visual tools like Concept Maps, and an entire section dedicated to Mind Mapping with children. I guarantee the information to make you a smarter, more productive, creative, and effective individual.

<u>Improve Memory, Concentration, Communication, Organization, Creativity, and Time Management with Mind Maps</u> by Ken Arthur

If you would like to learn other ways to enhance your mental performance, specifically in the area of memory, a great guide on the topic is:

Memory: Simple, Easy, and Fun Ways to Improve Memory by John Parker

Made in the USA
Middletown, DE
28 June 2016